THAILAND UNHINGED

FEDERICO FERRARA

THAILAND UNHINGED
THE DEATH OF THAI-STYLE DEMOCRACY

EQUINOX
PUBLISHING
JAKARTA KUALA LUMPUR

EQUINOX PUBLISHING (ASIA) PTE LTD
No 3, Shenton Way
#10-05 Shenton House
Singapore 068805

www.EquinoxPublishing.com

THAILAND UNHINGED
The Death of Thai-Style Democracy
by Federico Ferrara

ISBN: 978-979-3780-84-9

Second Equinox Edition 2011

Copyright © 2011 Federico Ferrara

Printed in the United States of America

1 3 5 7 9 10 8 6 4 2

All rights reserved. No part of this publication may be reproduced, stored in a retrieval system, or transmitted in any form or by any means, electronic, mechanical, photocopying, recording, or otherwise without the prior permission of Equinox Publishing.

For the dead, and the living.

CONTENTS

Foreword	9
Coups for Democracy	15
In Name of the Father	41
Tyranny of the Big Men	67
Thailand for Sale	95
Democracy, Thai-Style	119
Revolt of the Unholy	145
Twilight of the Idols	171

*Freedom is the freedom to say
that two plus two make four.
If that is granted, all else follows.*

—George Orwell
Nineteen Eighty-Four

FOREWORD

April 13, 2010 started out like most other days. I woke up, lit a cigarette, fixed a cup of espresso, and took a seat on the living-room couch of my small, rented apartment on Singapore's east side. As I had done almost every morning since the middle of March, I logged on to my computer and opened up the internet page that carried the People Channel's live video stream, broadcasting from the site of the Red Shirt rallies at Saphan Phan Fa and the Rajprasong intersection. It was just three days earlier that the military had tried unsuccessfully to disperse the rallies, causing the death of more than two dozen people. I cannot remember what, if anything, would prompt it, but on that day I was overtaken by the impulse to be there and experience, first hand, what had already become a historic event. Having taught the semester's last class just the day before, it would not be difficult to find a flight and a hotel room, even on a couple hours' notice. By mid-afternoon, I had landed in Bangkok, emptied out by the annual exodus of locals for the Songkhran festivities and the defection of foreign tourists kept away by the violence.

That was the last time I have traveled to Thailand, a country where I had spent a great deal of time over the previous several years. It will remain the last time for the foreseeable future. The trip itself did not trigger any sudden epiphany. It was only weeks later, after the Red Shirts were definitively crushed, that I would begin to reconcile myself to the idea that I should never again return to Thailand — at least, not until it is no longer a crime to speak of the nation's professed "father" in anything but the vaguest or most sycophantic terms.

I know for a fact that the people massacred by the military in April and May 2010 were none of the things the government said they were — not terrorists, not Maoists, not traitors, not drunken hooligans, not hired mobs, and not simpletons brainwashed by an exiled billionaire. The Red Shirts I met during that trip to Bangkok, and many trips before that, are just ordinary people. Not an especially ideological bunch, either — for the most part, these men and women are just sick of being told that choosing the country's leaders is a task best left to those blessed with status, riches, or good karma. They say they are fighting for "democracy," but for most of them democracy is perhaps less of an end than it is the means by which to affirm their dignity as equal citizens.

For the temerity of expressing aspirations every self-respecting human being harbors, and for having broken a few laws that are only invoked when it is convenient to do so, almost ninety of them were butchered on the streets of Bangkok, to the cheers of Thailand's privileged classes and the indifference of the rest of the world. Presented with the courage exhibited by so many of those men and women in the face of brute military force, I could not help but feel a strong measure of shame for having failed to speak out publicly about the institution — Thailand's monarchy — in whose name those ordinary people, like hundreds before them, had been murdered.

Like the overwhelming majority of the existing journalistic and scholarly work on Thailand, this book's first edition, published in February 2010, was aggressively self-censored in its treatment of core members of the Thai royal family and the role of the institution. In part, that was done to give the book a chance to reach the bulk of its potential readership in Thailand. For a variety of reasons, some not clear to me to this day, this never actually happened; to my knowledge, no copy of the book has ever seen the inside of a bookstore in Bangkok. More importantly, I self-censored because, like most people interested in Thai history, politics, or culture, I wanted to be able to continue traveling to Thailand without fear of being arrested and thrown in jail.

This new edition of *Thailand Unhinged* is not self-censored. At least with regard to the monarchy, it is the book I should have written last year — no coded language, no glossing over, no beating around the bush. Of course, there are certain trade-offs that the decision to refrain from visiting Thailand comports. These trade-offs vary according to one's individual circumstances and standards, so I do not begrudge anyone who has come to a different conclusion. For my decision to stay away is every bit as cowardly as theirs. Choosing to exercise freedom of speech over freedom of movement is, I suppose, the easy part. Somewhat more onerous are the limitations that telling a more complete story imposes on one's ability to actually *get* the complete story. Thankfully, from this standpoint at least, I am no anthropologist or ethnographer. And so while the ability to do my job is likely to suffer from the fact that I can no longer be there and talk to regular people to the same extent I did before, my research agenda can be easily adjusted on that basis. Whatever research I can no longer conduct in the field can be delegated to a research assistant hired for that purpose. Going forward, speaking my own mind will be delegated to no one.

One does not often get to do rewrites in this line of work. In fact, one of the best pieces of advice I ever received in graduate school was to never read my own work once it appears in print. This time, however, it was well worth putting myself through the invariably cringe-worthy experience, and take the opportunity to craft an all-around better product. From a stylistic viewpoint, I re-organized the work somewhat and amended some of the phrasing I had, in retrospect, come to find a bit awkward, gratuitous, or overly simplistic. From a more substantive perspective, writing a new edition presented a chance to further elaborate on some issues, or flesh out some of my views more explicitly. These kinds of edits affect various parts of the book, but it might be worth highlighting the most significant.

In the first edition of *Thailand Unhinged*, one of the main points I sought to convey was that Thailand's political conflict has both an elite dimension — a power struggle that has very little to do with "democracy" — as well as elements of a fight for the future of Thailand as a more or less democratic nation, at the heart of which are serious political, social, and economic grievances. This stands in contrast to narratives of the Thai crisis that see the conflict as either one or the other — as "a tale of two democracies," "a tale of two dictatorships," or a simpler "tale of democracy against dictatorship." On balance, the first edition's harsh treatment of Thaksin Shinawatra on the one hand, and the sympathetic treatment offered to the Red Shirts on the other, made the point clearly enough. But in retrospect I had come to find the articulation of the overall thesis to be exceedingly jumbled. This is perhaps the consequence of the fact that the book was assembled from text written at different times. And so the passages originally written before the Red Shirts had become the force that they are now emphasized the elite dimension to an extent with which I have become somewhat uncomfortable. The new edition, while making the same basic argument, seeks to do so in a more organic fashion.

While I was thankful for the opportunity to make these revisions, none are of such import to justify the release of a new version of *Thailand Unhinged*. The main reason behind this new release is rather the ambition to keep the work current in the face of the historic events, many of them tragic but some decidedly less so, that have taken place in Thailand over the past year. The first edition was rushed to print because, like many others, I expected that something big was going to happen, and hoped the book might contribute to making sense of what was about to unfold. But nobody quite knew *what* was going to happen or what its import would be. As it turns out, what did transpire is not only significant enough to warrant a major update, reflected in the addition of some thirty pages of text, but also helps provide the entire account with a more definitive, less open-ended narrative — ideally, making the book's conclusions less perishable over time (if still, quite possibly, dead wrong).

Even before giving any serious consideration to the possibility of working on a new edition, I had interpreted the 2010 demonstrations staged by the Red Shirts as marking the "death" of "Thai-Style Democracy." This interpretation falls somewhere in between the one offered by Chris Baker, who spoke of "the death of deference" at about the same time, and that of David Streckfuss, whose newly released book speaks of the coming death of "Thainess" — an ideology he aptly describes as a rather odious form of nihilism. Either way, while the first edition sought to illustrate the workings of "Thai-Style Democracy" and evaluate the mounting threats to its continued existence, this new and improved version of *Thailand Unhinged* concludes with an account of its (presumed) death. The country's political conflict, to be sure, remains far from over. But a sharp break with the past now seems inevitable, in light of the history the Red Shirts made in 2010. As John Kenneth Galbraith might have put it, the end has come but is not yet in sight.

—FEDERICO FERRARA
Hong Kong, February 28, 2011

We know that no one ever seizes power
with the intention of relinquishing it.
Power is not a means, it is an end.
One does not establish a dictatorship in
order to safeguard a revolution;
one makes the revolution in order to
establish the dictatorship.

—GEORGE ORWELL
Nineteen Eighty-Four

ONE

COUPS FOR DEMOCRACY

> They call it a 'democratic coup d'état,'
> see. You have to have lots of coups d'état.
> Otherwise it isn't a democracy.
>
> —Khamsing Srinawk[1]

The military made its move on September 19, 2006. Ominously foreshadowing that something big was about to go down, television stations abruptly cut out of scheduled programming and played soothing, ready-made slideshows bearing still images of the royal family, at times accompanied by music composed by His Majesty the King. Shortly thereafter, CNN reported that tanks were advancing through Bangkok, rolling down Rachadamnoen Avenue in the direction of the Government House. The capital city — a megalopolis of ten million people — was taken with derisive ease, in a matter of minutes. A few tanks and a busload of special forces moved in from Lopburi was all it took for the army to re-take control of the entire country. Prime Minister Thaksin Shinawatra, hours away from speaking to the United Nations General Assembly, feigned outrage and surprise. But he had long been forewarned.

---

1. Khamsing Srinawk, "The Politician,'" in *The Politician and Other Stories* (Chiang Mai: Silkworm Books, 2001).

Two months before the coup, an article in *The Nation* bore what even back then looked like an obvious sign that time was running out on Thaksin's administration. Privy Council President Prem Tinsulanonda — a retired general, former Prime Minister, and now King Bhumibol Adulyadej's seniormost *consigliere* — was reported to have publicly reminded a group of graduating cadets that the loyalty of the military should rest with the King, not the elected government.[2] In a country with Thailand's history, the meaning of Prem's words could not be lost on the Prime Minister. Indeed, it was reported in the aftermath of the coup that Thaksin had loaded two Thai Airways International flights with 114 suitcases and large trunks of "personal effects" upon leaving the country — all that for what was supposed to have been a two-week journey to Europe and North America.[3]

Cheered in Bangkok and unencumbered by any hint of active popular opposition, the generals solicitously apologized for the "inconvenience" caused, promised to return the country to democracy within a year, and for good measure gave everyone a day off. The edicts that suspended the 1997 constitution and banned all political activities were accompanied by the instruction that soldiers keep smiling in public.[4] Three days later, a pro-democracy demonstration was held in the busy shopping complex at Siam Center; banners read "No to Coup and No to Thaksin." It was attended by an oceanic crowd estimated at twenty to a hundred people.[5] On September 30, a lone protester badly injured himself after crashing his taxi into a tank. The reliably servile *Bangkok Post* snidely reported the incident in its online breaking news section under the headline: "Tank 1, Taxi 0 in Apparent Protest." Democracy had died in Thailand. Few, however, seemed to mourn its passing.

---

2. "Military Must Back King," *The Nation*, July 15, 2006.
3. "All Projects Face Probe," *The Nation*, September 25, 2006.
4. "A 'Model' Coup," *The Nation*, October 2, 2006.
5. Apiradee Treerutkuarkul, "Rally Draws 20 Anti-Coup Protesters," *Bangkok Post*, September 23, 2006.

Indeed, it was argued at the time that the army did not kill democracy. The generals had merely euthanized it, ending its long, painful agony by bringing Thaksin's elected dictatorship to a deservedly ignominious close. Thaksin, after all, had already eviscerated democratic institutions, imposing a measure of repression and social control more reminiscent of an authoritarian regime than a representative government in a free country.

In five years at the helm, Thaksin had systematically subjected dissenting voices to police brutality, legal harassment, and a relentless smear campaign that portrayed them as anarchists and enemies of the nation. He had revived repressive legislation granting the police expansive powers to search and interrogate suspects. He had moved to assert editorial control over the television channels owned by the state. He had routinely pressured the print media to give favorable coverage through threats of legal action and the manipulation of the advertising budget of state-owned enterprises. And he had vanquished independent bodies like the Election Commission, the National Counter Corruption Commission, and the National Human Rights Commission through carrots, sticks, and a wave of partisan appointments.

More shamefully still, in 2003 Thaksin had launched a "War on Drugs" through which he vowed to eradicate drug trafficking within ninety days. Between February and April 2003, scores of people were caught up in a flurry of killings and extra-judicial executions. In late 2007, a representative of Thailand's Office of Narcotics Control Board put the death toll at over 2,500, possibly as many as 1,400 of whom had nothing at all to do with drugs.[6] A few months thereafter, in early 2008, an investigative panel appointed by the junta estimated that 1,370 people somehow connected to the drug trade were killed during the campaign. An additional fifty-four deaths were classified as "extra-judicial executions," while 571 inci-

---

6. "Most of Those Killed in War on Drug Not Involved in Drug," *The Nation*, November 27, 2007.

dents of murder were found to have "no identified causes."[7] Whether the government's campaign made much of a dent in the lucrative narcotics trade is not altogether clear. Drug abuse was reported on the rise in 2005.[8]

As if that was not enough, Thaksin's heavy hand had also helped inflame long-dormant ethnic tensions in Thailand's Muslim-majority southern provinces of Pattani, Yala, and Narathiwat. Insurgent offensives that targeted army bases and government schools in early 2004 were followed by the government's brutal reprisals. The military and the police were cited in a number of episodes of torture, kidnapping, and murder of activists and suspected insurgents. Voices of dissent like those of human rights advocate Somchai Neelaphaijit were forever silenced. On April 28, 113 people were killed in incidents that culminated with the massacre of twenty-eight lightly-armed men who had barricaded themselves inside the Kru Ze mosque in Pattani. The following October, the military caused the death by suffocation of seventy-eight among the hundreds of people who had been loaded onto military trucks during a peaceful protest at Tak Bai. By 2006, what had once been effectively contained to a low-intensity conflict characterized by sporadic episodes of minor violence erupted into a full-scale insurgency, the daily attacks on the representatives and the symbols of the state leaving hundreds dead in their wake.

Thailand, of course, has a long history of "democratic" coups d'état — having famously drifted in and out of military dictatorship ever since a group of mostly young, foreign-educated military officers and high-ranking civil servants overthrew the absolute monarchy in 1932. Even back then, the

---

7. An unofficial English translation of the "Preliminary Report" issued by the "Independent Committee for the Study and Analysis of the Formulation and Implementation of the Narcotic Suppression Policy" is downloadable from the website Prachatai: http://www.prachatai.com/english/node/551.
8. "Poll Finding: Drug Abuse on the Rise," *The Nation*, March 20, 2005.

men who usurped King Prajadhipok's absolute powers had announced that Thailand (then Siam) would embrace democracy, the stuff of civilized nations. In due course, that is. While some of the Promoters of the 1932 Revolution — Pridi Banomyong foremost among them — were serious about eventually transforming the country into a liberal democracy, the leaders of the People's Party (*khana ratsadon*) also had good reason to fear that the scarce "readiness" of the Thai people would land them out of power.

Not content with stacking half of the newly instituted National Assembly with their own appointees, the Promoters banned political parties from contesting legislative elections. As the military faction gradually asserted its dominance over the People's Party, moreover, the government tightened the screws on freedom of expression, assembly, and association — increasingly, the People's Party arrogated the role of sole protector of the constitution and true representative of "the people." Even a timid, unorganized opposition was too much for the new regime to bear, judging from the number of critics who were arrested, subjected to show trials, banished to faraway lands, or summarily executed. By the onset of World War II, the country had all but completed its reversal into military dictatorship.

With the end of World War II came new hopes that the promise of democracy would finally be fulfilled. The government led by Field Marshal Phibul Songkhram — who shared more than passing ideological affinities with the Japanese occupiers he enabled — was jettisoned as Japan approached defeat. In the aftermath of the war, in 1946, a new constitution and a generally more liberal environment led to the registration of political parties — among them, the Democrat Party — and the election of a new National Assembly finally devoid of appointed deputies. Phibul, however, stormed back onto the scene in 1947, staging a coup that abrogated the new constitution and invalidated the results of the election. In the tumultuous decade that ensued, Phibul survived two violent coup attempts (in 1949 and 1951) and saw his powers curtailed by the 1951 "Radio Coup" staged by top brass in the military and the police, who sought to thwart the rise of the increasingly vocal National Assembly. While Phibul remained in office, Field Marshal Sarit Thanarat and Police Director-General Phao Sriyanond forced the re-introduction of the 1932 charter and its system of "tutelary democracy."

Ironically, when Phibul was definitively deposed, in 1957, the pretext for the coup staged by Sarit Thanarat was that the elections held in February had been rigged. Not only did Sarit nominally belong to the same party that benefited from the alleged fraud; Sarit himself had much less of a taste for democracy than his predecessor. Phibul, for his part, seemed genuinely ambivalent about democratic reforms. On the one hand, he saw in democratic elections a means to establish a power base outside the military and the bureaucratic elite. It was no doubt the need for legitimation that motivated Phibul to call for a vote upon returning to power in 1947. And it was likely in an attempt to extricate himself from Phao and Sarit that he pushed for a skeletal Political Parties Act (introduced in 1955) and unexpectedly liberalized political speech upon his return from a trip to the United States and the United Kingdom.[9] On the other hand, Phibul was too distrustful of any form of organized opposition that threatened to limit his own power and not confident enough of his pull with the electorate to decisively follow through.[10]

Sarit had no such qualms. With his *autogolpe*, less than a year later, came the requisite abrogation of the constitution, a renewed ban on political parties, and the beginning of an era

---

9. Contemporaneous accounts suggest that Phibul was impressed with the degree of independence that leaders like Winston Churchill and Dwight Eisenhower enjoyed thanks to their electoral popularity. See David A. Wilson and Herbert P. Phillips, "Elections and Parties in Thailand," *Far Eastern Survey* 27 (1958): 113-119.

10. Kramol Tongdhamachart, *Toward a Political Party Theory in Thai Perspective* (Singapore: Institute of Southeast Asian Studies Occasional Paper No. 68, 1982), pp. 8-9.

of "despotic paternalism" — a time during which the government's cruelty and heavy-handedness was only matched by the prodigious thievery of its leader.[11] Most political activities were proscribed and harshly repressed by Sarit's iron-fisted dictatorship; when his liver finally gave out to a lifetime of boozing, his worthy successor, Thanom Kittikachorn, turned out to be no less reactionary or barbaric. At least until Thanom deemed it prudent to schedule a new round of voting in 1969, in a tragically bungled attempt to consolidate his position, Sarit and Thanom did not look to democratic elections for legitimation. They rather devoted themselves to the restoration of the monarchy's mystique and power. It was during this time that the foundations were laid for the crown's resurgent popularity, resulting eventually in King Bhumibol's apotheosis.

Whereas introducing, restoring, or otherwise saving democracy has been cited as a justification for many of the plentiful coups that have forcibly, if often bloodlessly, removed a succession of Thai governments since 1932, real democracy has rather more often come to Thailand after torrents of civilian blood streamed copiously through the streets of Bangkok.

The first such incident was sparked by the repression of student demonstrations carried out in October 1973 by the "Three Tyrants" — Field Marshal Thanom Kittikachorn, Field Marshal Prapat Charusathien, and Colonel Narong Kittikachorn — two years after Thanom had dissolved the National Assembly and voided the results of elections he had himself "won" in 1969. By the time half a million people took to the streets on October 13, the more immediate demands for the release of activists arrested a week earlier had grown into more sweeping calls for democratic change. In a characteristically measured response, on October 14 the military began firing into the crowds, gunning down over a hundred unarmed demonstrators. Faced with the prospect of still more

---

11. See Thak Chaloemtiarana, *Thailand: The Politics of Despotic Paternalism* (Chiang Mai: Silkworm Books, 2007[1979]), pp. 223-224.

massive, angrier demonstrations, Thanom called for the imposition of martial law, but was denied by Army Commander Krit Srivara. Thanks to the public intervention of King Bhumibol — characteristically, too late to save the students' lives, but just in time to aggrandize his own status — the Three Tyrants resigned and fled the country.

The elections organized in 1975 are generally recognized as the first genuinely competitive elections held in the country's history. Not only was competition in this round of voting not hamstrung by the stringent restrictions traditionally imposed on political speech, assembly, and association; this time, no "government party" was there to parlay an outsized financial advantage and the exclusive control of the state into an all too predictable triumph at the polls.

Thailand's 1975 elections, however, bore all the hallmarks of the competition for contributors, candidates, and votes in the absence of strong, national party organizations. The government appointed by the King in 1973 to see the country through the transition was based on a coalition of no less than fourteen political parties. Having little territorial coverage and no organization in the districts, such parties chose to rely on two formidable local figures to mobilize votes in rural Thailand. To be sure, both had played some role in previous contests, but their support was only rendered more crucial by the increased competitiveness of national elections. First, parties enlisted typically unsavory characters known as *chao pho*, or "godfathers" — most commonly Sino-Thai provincial bosses who had made veritable fortunes in Thailand's vast submerged economy.[12] *Chao pho* had much to offer an aspiring officeholder. They commanded the services of hundreds of young men and intricate organizational networks such as those in place to operate underground lotteries; as such, they

---

12. See, for instance, Pasuk Phongpaichit, Sungsidh Piriyarangsan, and Nualnoi Treerat, *Guns, Girls, Gambling, and Ganja: Thailand's Illegal Economy and Public Policy* (Chiang Mai: Silkworm Books, 1998).

were in a unique position to dispense patronage services to constituents on behalf of politicians. All they wanted in return was protection from the law. They were granted nothing less.

Second, budding political parties organized multi-layered networks of canvassers — or *hua khanaen* — who could deliver votes through a mixture of persuasion and moral authority (village teachers, temple abbots), coercion (common criminals), fraud (government officials) and vote-buying (all of the above). While government parties once had quasi-monopolistic access to capable *hua khanaen*, the competition was much fiercer now that no surefire winner could be identified *ex ante* as guaranteeing a meaningful return on the investment of time, money, and reputation that any local notable would have to put into the election of a given candidate. The situation, moreover, was rendered more chaotic by the fact that economic growth and the plentiful development funds that had made their way into the periphery since the days of the Vietnam War had created a whole new class of powerful notabilities — especially those connected to local businesses with access to government contracts.

The 1975 elections returned a highly splintered House of Representatives where as many as twenty-two political parties — most of them mere electoral vehicles for politicians with a strong local base — occupied parliamentary seats. It fell to Social Action Party leader Kukrit Pramoj to piece together a coalition government with a chance to survive a confidence vote. The painstaking process of cajoling so many different parties, as well as the manifold factions thereof, ultimately resulted in the formation of a limp, sixteen-party executive. An elaborate system of quotas was introduced, whereby each party and faction would receive a share of portfolios and undersecretaries commensurate with its size.

It has been pointed out that this method of dividing the spoils of government — born of necessity — set the Thai political system on the path to the kind of extreme fragmentation and instability it has exhibited ever since.[13] Most importantly, perhaps, it created an incentive for the already independent-minded members of parliament (MPs) to form factions that could trade their participation in the government's legislative majority for a cabinet post. The most ambitious and resourceful representatives led factions held together by their ability to bankroll the campaigns of less affluent followers; once in government, the faction leader would use the office to recoup his investment. The logic by which both factions and parties operated, moreover, was such to generate high levels of instability at both levels. Within factions, individual MPs could shift their support to whomever would pay the highest price for it. And, within parties, because most factions commanded their own finances and electoral organizations, little pressure could be exerted on them to exhibit any level of party discipline. In fact, all that bound different factions together in a single party was the expectation that the party would be invited to join the government. Accordingly, a party out of power could well expect to break up, as its factions scrambled to find alternative routes to all-important executive posts.

Barely a year into its term, Kukrit's government collapsed. New elections were held in April 1976, but voters returned an assembly only marginally less fractious than the one elected the year before. This time, nineteen parties won seats in the House. The weak government formed by Democrat Party leader Seni Pramoj survived a mere six months.

Thailand's first real experience under a fully democratic regime ended much the same way it began — in tragedy and bloodshed. Though the democratic governments that ruled Thailand between 1973 and 1976 were not short of notable achievements,[14] their extreme fragmentation largely imped-

---

13. See James Ockey, *Making Democracy: Leadership, Class, Gender, and Political Participation in Thailand* (Chiang Mai: Silkworm Books, 2004).

14. See, for instance, Benedict R. Anderson, "Elections and Participation in Three Southeast Asian Countries," in *The Politics of Elections in Southeast Asia*, ed. Robert H. Taylor (Cambridge Univer-

ed decisive action on the most pressing issues of the day — among them, increasingly bitter labor disputes, a restive student movement in Bangkok, and the communist guerrilla in the Northeast. It did not help matters that royalist, civilian vigilantes and the military embarked on a sustained campaign of bombings and assassinations targeting rural activists and leftist politicians, undermining the public's confidence in the ability of a democratic government to keep the peace.

The return to Thailand of former strongman Thanom Kittikachorn, in the fall of 1976, sparked a new wave of student demonstrations that were once again savagely repressed. In this instance, however, the troops largely stood by as organized paramilitary thugs such as the Red Gaurs and the Village Scouts slaughtered dozens of Thammasat University students and mutilated their corpses. His Majesty the King — who, after all, generously patronized both groups before and after this incident — said nothing publicly, but quickly endorsed the inevitable military coup that followed.

The National Administrative Reform Council, as the new junta called itself, ruthlessly pursued leftists suspected of communist sympathies as well as any voice clamoring for a return to democracy. Thousands of students and intellectuals fled the country or retreated to the jungles — joining forces with the communist insurgency in Isan. Hundreds more were arrested on trumped-up charges and tried in military tribunals. The new strongman, Supreme Court judge Tanin Kraivichien, was empowered by the new constitution to exercise near-absolute rule, checked only by an appointed legislature of handpicked military and public administration officials. By 1977, Tanin had become so unpopular — even the military found the cruelty and paranoid extremism of his regime distasteful — that the army deposed him in yet another bloodless coup.

In the decade that followed, Thailand was ruled by a hybrid regime dominated by the palace and the military but

---

sity Press, 1996), p. 18.

supported by democratically elected legislatures.[15] New elections were held in 1979 after the promulgation of the country's latest "permanent" constitution. Difficulties in putting together a coalition government were ultimately overcome with the appointment of General Prem Tinsulanonda, who ended up serving as Prime Minister between 1980 and 1988.

Though not terribly consequential to the exercise of real political power, elections held during that period were hotly contested, especially as the positions of member of parliament and cabinet minister became potentially more lucrative in a context of fast-paced economic growth. If, as of the 1970s, seventy-five percent of the members of parliament were estimated to have received kickbacks from development projects or direct cash payments in return for their support of a party,[16] the use of public office for private gain was transformed into a booming cottage industry in the 1980s. One grim measure of the newfound competitiveness of national elections is offered by Benedict Anderson, who notes that political assassinations in the 1980s were increasingly related to the races for parliamentary seats.[17] Eliminating rival candidates became much more commonplace than it had been in the past. So did the practice of taking out *hua khanaen* who hogged too large a share of the resources disbursed by candidates while failing to deliver a commensurate number of votes.[18]

---

15. The classic statement on the "semi-democracy" of the time is in Clark D. Neher, "Thailand in 1987: Semi-Successful Semi-Democracy," *Asian Survey* 28 (1988): 192-201. See also Chai-Anan Samudavanija, "Thailand: A Stable Semi-Democracy," in Larry Diamond, Juan Linz, and Seymour Martin Lipset (eds.), *Democracy in Developing Countries* (London: Lynne Rienner Publishers, 1990), 271-312.
16. Pasuk Phongpaichit and Sungsidh Piriyarangsan, *Corruption and Democracy in Thailand* (Chiang Mai: Silkworm Books, 1994), p. 3.
17. Benedict R. Anderson, "Murder and Progress in Modern Siam," *New Left Review* 181(1990): 33-48.
18. Alan Klima, *The Funeral Casino: Meditation, Massacre, and Exchange with the Dead in Thailand* (Princeton, NJ: Princeton Uni-

After the 1988 elections, Prem declined to serve another term as Prime Minister and took a seat on King Bhumibol's Privy Council. For the first time in over a decade, elections would matter to the formation of a new government. The prime ministerial post was assumed by Chatichai Choonhavan, leader of Chat Thai — the largest party in the newly elected National Assembly. Propped up by neither the military nor the palace — both repeatedly expressed their displeasure with the Prime Minister — the new government was to survive entirely on its own power. But given the fragmentation of Thailand's legislature, Chatichai's only hope to put together a durable coalition was to indulge the seemingly limitless appetite for personal gain and political patronage characteristic of the main parties and factions.

What might have seemed at first as the dawn of a new era of parliamentarism and democracy in Thailand — now finally ruled by a government whose authority derived exclusively from the mandate it won electorally — was brought to an abrupt end in February 1991. Citing the intolerable corruption of Chatichai's "buffet cabinet" and the presence of many "unusually wealthy" politicians in its midst, General Suchinda Kraprayoon and his National Peace-Keeping Council (NPKC) seized power, promising reforms, investigations, and a swift return to democracy. Meanwhile, the military wasted no time abrogating the constitution and dissolving the National Assembly — the customary measures called for by these familiar circumstances. The public acquiesced. King Bhumibol said nothing officially, but let it be known via Suchinda that the coup-makers had his blessing, at least so long as they did not "let the people down."

The events that followed offer a poignant demonstration that coups in Thailand have nothing at all to do with restoring democracy.[19] Once in control, the NPKC did everything

---

versity Press, 2004), p. 96.
19. David Murray's book *Angels and Devils* is required reading for anyone interested in the circumstances surrounding the 1991 coup

in its power to stay there, notwithstanding the veneer of democratic legitimacy it sought to establish through competent administration and competitive elections. One of the NPKC's first orders of business was to appoint Prime Minister Anand Panyarachun, a widely respected former ambassador most considered genuinely *super partes*. Anand was given wide discretion to reassure foreign investors and embark on a sweeping reform of the country's economy. To this day, his technocratic government is often said to have been the best the country has ever known. But the scope of its activities was severely limited. On matters other than the economy, the NPKC was unmistakably calling the shots, determined as it was to entrench its rule.

The military's determination to install Suchinda in the Prime Minister's office, presumably to serve in much the same capacity Prem had in the 1980s, was most evident in its stewardship of the process that ushered in a new "democratic" constitution. Two proposals, in particular, were most obviously designed for the NPKC to continue to rule well beyond the upcoming elections. First, the NPKC itself was to appoint a 270-member Senate endowed with similar prerogatives as the House of Representatives. Second, the constitution contained no provision requiring that the Prime Minister be drawn from the ranks of the people's representatives. Few believed Suchinda's protestations to the contrary: the door was kept open for himself or another general to assume the position. And so the basic institutional infrastructure that would allow the military to restore Thailand to a semi-democracy — or, as *The Nation* put it back then, "a dictatorship in the guise of democracy" — was firmly in place. All this was apparent to independent print media outlets, non-governmental organizations, and opposition parties that vigorously opposed

---

and the chain of events that led to a new democratic transition in 1992. David Murray, *Angels and Devils: Thai Politics from February 1991 to September 1992 — A Struggle for Democracy?* (Bangkok: Orchid Press, 1996).

the charter. But the opposition fizzled when the NPKC agreed to make minor changes to the proposed draft and, especially, when His Majesty the King stepped in to urge the public to go along with the document, on the grounds that "any rule can be changed."

If the new charter made it possible for the military to stay in power, the NPKC's actions on the electoral front were designed to guarantee that this would be the case. A new party, Samakkhitham, was created in the hope that it would form the core of Suchinda's legislative majority. Through an aggressive recruitment campaign, Samakkhitham enlisted the support of wealthy contributors as well as eighty former MPs and eleven former cabinet ministers — most of them based in northern and northeastern constituencies. Each seems to have been offered an initial 500,000 baht, the equivalent of $20,000 at that time's exchange rate, for their campaigns, with more to be disbursed at a later stage.[20] But it was plain to the top brass that this alone would not be enough to secure a majority in the House. The best the NPKC could hope for was a strong showing by Samakkhitham and the formation of a coalition government with other parties.

Suchinda's options were limited. Some of the largest parties — the Democrats as well as the New Aspiration Party and Palang Dharma — had defined themselves in opposition to military rule and more or less vehemently denounced the actions of the junta. Awkwardly, the only parties available to join Samakkhitham's coalition were those the NPKC had overthrown the year before — Chat Thai and Social Action — with the pretext of saving democracy. Apart from the obvious hypocrisy of forging any such alliance, the move posed serious practical problems. The key obstacle was that some of these parties' more powerful politicians were under investigation by the newly instituted Assets Evaluation Committee for the "unusual wealth" they had allegedly amassed while in office; all faced a possible lifetime ban from elected posts.

---
20. Ibid., p. 41.

But the generals took care of that. Some Chat Thai and Social Action Party leaders who accepted to cooperate with the military were exonerated for lack of evidence. Then, the provisional charter was amended so as to allow the ten politicians whom the AEC had found guilty of misappropriating funds to appeal their sentences, thereby enabling them to pursue elected office for the foreseeable future. It would take years for the Appeals Court to review and adjudicate their cases.

In the space of fourteen months, Thailand had come full circle. The NPKC had come to power promising to clean up the system. It aggressively went after (some) corrupt politicians and confiscated their assets. To cling to power, however, it had little option but to let the same people off the hook, return them to their lucrative posts, and adopt their very electoral practices. The result was that Thailand would have much the same government it had before, albeit with the added luxury of the military back in charge. The farcical nature of this turn of events was not lost on Suchinda, who after the March 1992 elections stated his refusal to serve as Prime Minister in any government that included officials the AEC had found culpable of plundering state coffers. Eventually, though, even the strongman had to bow down to the iron laws of Thai politics. Suchinda formed a five-party executive that included eleven politicians initially accused of being "unusually wealthy" as well as many others with shady backgrounds and dubious associations.[21] By resorting to the same electoral strategies it ostensibly sought to stamp out — entirely reasonable from a purely instrumental standpoint, given their effectiveness — the military had sown the seeds of its own government's corruption, paralysis, and instability.

Far from definitively putting the issue to rest, Suchinda's formal assumption of the Prime Minister's job galvanized the opposition. The small protests that followed Suchinda's appointment gave way, in early May, to a rapid crescendo of

---

21. Ibid., p. 125.

street demonstrations led by retired Major-General Chamlong Srimuang, leader of the small party Palang Dharma and former governor of Bangkok. Chamlong went on a hunger strike on May 4 — announcing that he would fast until the day he died or Suchinda resigned. Demonstrations in Sanam Luang — a sun-scorched grass field nestled between the Thammasat University campus and the Temple of the Emerald Buddha — attracted eighty thousand people on May 4 and about a hundred and fifty thousand on May 8. The protesters only agreed to put further demonstrations on hiatus when the government announced it was prepared to negotiate the very changes to the constitution they had been clamoring for all along.

Predictably, that promise turned out to be a ruse to break the opposition's momentum. Faced with a coalition government little inclined to agree to any meaningful reform, new protests were staged up and down Rachadamnoen Avenue between Sanam Luang and the imposing Democracy Monument on May 17. As many as two hundred thousand people — from slum dwellers all the way up the social ladder to mobile-phone wielding corporate executives — attended the rallies. By early morning on May 18, following sporadic clashes between stone-throwing demonstrators and police, the government had declared a state of emergency and moved to crack down on the protesters. In what appeared to be the methodical execution of a well-orchestrated plan, the police and the army alternated between firing warning shots in the air and discharging their automatic weapons directly into the crowds of unarmed demonstrators. Pitched battles continued throughout the day on May 18, until on the following day, the army captured the Royal Hotel, savagely beating the demonstrators who had taken shelter in the last bastion of democratic resistance on Rachadamnoen Avenue. By the evening of May 19, the military was back in control. Dozens of people lay dead — many shot in the back while attempting to flee, some executed with bullets to the back of the head. And another confrontation was looming at Ramkhamhaeng University, where those determined to fight on had regrouped on May 20.

The turning point came that evening, when King Bhumibol summoned Suchinda and Chamlong for a royal audience that was to be televised worldwide. As the Prime Minister and the leader of the opposition meekly prostrated before him, the King downplayed the significance of the fight over an already "reasonable" constitution and said nothing of the fact that Suchinda had presided, just hours earlier, over the massacre of dozens of innocent people. The King rather characterized the crisis as a personal vendetta and urged the two to "sit down and face the facts in a conciliatory manner." Chamlong, who had been under arrest, was released by the authorities the next day. Suchinda resigned three days later, but only after securing the King's signature on a decree granting blanket amnesty to everyone involved in the events of May 17-20. On May 26, the constitution was changed according to the opposition's wishes. And, on June 10, Anand Panyarachun was tapped to serve another brief term as interim Prime Minister. New elections were only three months away.

The third coming of democracy in Thailand initially turned out to be much like the first and the second. At least in the print media, the campaign for the September 1992 elections was portrayed as a fight between "angels" and "devils" — the "angels" being the pro-democracy parties that had been behind the demonstrations (Democrats, Palang Dharma, and New Aspiration), the "devils" being the surviving parties among those that had supported Suchinda through the events of "Black May" — Chat Thai, Social Action, and Prachakorn Thai above all, plus the newly assembled Chat Pattana of deposed Prime Minister Chatichai. Samakkhitham in the meantime had imploded, its remnants swallowed up by Chat Thai. But for hype about angels and devils, the September 1992 elections were entirely analogous to those of years past. The legislature returned by the 1992 contests was just as fragmented and factionalized as it had been throughout the 1980s. The three angelic parties — Democrats, New Aspiration, and Palang Dharma, now joined by the smaller Solidarity party — won a narrow majority in the House, taking 185 seats. The remaining 175 seats were shared by seven other parties, the largest of which were Chat Thai and Chat Pattana.

The horse trading that took place after the elections evinced a political landscape far more fluid than the apocalyptic terms in which the media described the campaign might have suggested. Democrat leader Chuan Leekpai formed a coalition government that included Social Action, the least devilish of the parties that had supported Suchinda through the massacres just four months earlier. Unsurprisingly, Chuan's government failed to serve out its term — forced to resign in 1995 after Palang Dharma withdrew its support in a vain attempt to avert an ultimately fatal internal split. By that time, Chuan's majority had already withstood the defection of General Chavalit Yongchaiyudh's New Aspiration Party.

When new elections were called in 1995, many factions and their MPs were characteristically on the auction block. The most successful at chipping away candidates from other parties were Chat Thai and the Democrats, who fielded a number of incumbent MPs in excess of the number of seats they commanded in the House. Reportedly, some candidates were offered upwards of ten million baht ($400,000) to switch parties.[22] The 1995 elections brought to power a government headed by Chat Thai's new leader Barnharn Silpa-archa and supported by a ragtag assemblage of former "angel" and "devil" parties now united in their pursuit of the spoils of power. Barnharn's helplessly incompetent "mafia cabinet" lasted a mere fifteen months. In advance of the elections held in 1996, it was New Aspiration that bought the most candidates on the open market, running as many as sixty-one incumbents from the ranks of other parties in addition to the fifty-seven

---

22. David Murray, "The 1995 National Elections in Thailand: A Step Back for Democracy?," *Asian Survey* 36(1996): 361-375.

it could already count on.[23] Having precipitated the government's collapse, having forced the dissolution of parliament, and having subsequently managed to win a plurality of seats, it was now Chavalit's turn to form a new government.

It took the usual blend of choice and chance, purposeful design and unintended consequences, to shake up long-standing patterns of political competition in the late 1990s. The first major change was in the country's institutional architecture. Following the 1996 elections, after years of much talk but little action, a compromise was reached on the procedural rules that would govern the complete overhaul of Thailand's constitution. Chavalit's government allowed a ninety-nine-member Constitution Drafting Assembly to be impaneled. The document it produced was approved by the National Assembly the following year.

The 1997 constitution re-designed several of Thailand's key political institutions. The legislature was rendered more "democratic" by replacing the appointed Senate with an upper chamber whose members were to be elected at the provincial level on a non-partisan basis. The size of the House of Representatives was increased to five hundred deputies. All candidates were now required to have bachelor's degrees to stand for election. Voting was made compulsory, while an independent Election Commission was given wide-ranging authority to investigate allegations of fraud and vote-buying, disqualify candidates found to have committed the gravest infractions, and ban the most egregiously corrupt politicians from elected office. The constitution included the explicit recognition of forty human rights — many unsanctioned in previous charters — as well as provisions guaranteeing Thai citizens greater protection from warrantless searches and seizures. A number of independent agencies were instituted as a means to fight corruption, human rights violations, and other abuses of power.

---

23. David Murray, "The Thai Parliamentary Elections of 1995 and 1996," *Electoral Studies* 16(1997): 379-427.

If the new constitution reshaped the legal framework within which political competition took place, the financial crisis that brought Thailand's once-buoyant economy to its knees in 1997, quickly spreading to much of East and Southeast Asia, completely revolutionized the dynamics of political competition. Repeated promises to the contrary notwithstanding, Chavalit's government responded to sustained attacks on the Thai baht and the consequent depletion of the country's currency reserves by unpegging the national currency from its fixed, 25 baht for $1 exchange rate. In one year, the baht lost over half of its value, destroying some of the wealth built during the expansion of the previous fifteen years. The banking sector collapsed. Companies that had accumulated significant foreign debt went bankrupt. Eight hundred thousand people lost their jobs as the unemployment rate tripled. The stock market plunged. The gross domestic product shrank by ten percent. And three million more people were now poor.[24]

The crisis dealt a severe blow to national leaders and organizations, creating opportunities for new ones to take their place. The flimsy coalition that supported Chavalit's government was the first casualty. Four months after floating the baht, Chavalit was forced to resign and was replaced by a new government headed by Chuan Leekpai. Though ultimately successful in engineering Thailand's economic recovery, Chuan and his cabinet were deeply unpopular because of their association with the International Monetary Fund. Characteristically, the crisis had been blamed on the twin bogeymen of international capitalism and globalization, so the structural adjustment policies that the IMF attached as a condition for bailing out the Thai economy through a $17.5 billion loan were viewed as yet another unwanted imposition from the same actors responsible for the crisis. With the decline of New Aspiration and the Democrats, the party system of old was left in shambles. And its re-organization was now to take

---

24. See Pasuk Phongpaichit and Chris Baker, *Thailand's Crisis* (Chiang Mai: Silkworm Books, 2000).

place under a much different set of rules.

It is in this context of upheaval and growing mistrust of the country's elites that the stalled political career of Thaksin Shinawatra accelerated to meteoric speed. Thaksin had risen to national prominence as a telecommunications magnate, having made a fortune by securing government concessions over the booming markets for mobile phones and pagers thanks to well-placed contacts in Chatichai's "buffet cabinet" (1988-1991). By the early 1990s, Thaksin had become inordinately wealthy; his firms were marvelously profitable, their value had multiplied several times over in the stock market. Thaksin's interest in politics was natural. Given that government concessions are typically awarded and renewed through an entirely political process, it is no surprise that Thaksin got involved when Thailand seemed destined to undertake the road to economic liberalization charted by Anand during his first tenure as Prime Minister in 1991. Thaksin formally entered the fray in 1994, becoming Foreign Minister in the first Chuan government (1992-1995) under the ministerial quota set aside for Palang Dharma.[25]

Palang Dharma's subsequent disintegration took place largely as a result of Thaksin's involvement. The party had built its image as an incorruptible organization inspired by Buddhist principles and administered by people whose lifestyle appeared to embody that very ethos. Thaksin, by contrast, was the quintessential "crony capitalist," having made his money via backroom deals and personal connections. His invitation to assume a cabinet post split the party, resulting in Palang Dharma's withdrawal from the coalition and the consequent collapse of Chuan's government. Now leader of the party following Chamlong Srimuang's retirement, Thaksin was elected to the House in 1995 and was given the position

---

25. Much of the historical detail discussed in this section on Thaksin's career in business and politics is drawn from Pasuk Phongpaichit and Chris Baker, *Thaksin* (Chiang Mai: Silkworm Books, 2009).

of Deputy Prime Minister. With Thaksin at the helm, Palang Dharma suffered a precipitous decline. The party had its legislative contingent slashed by half in 1995 and virtually disappeared from the scene in 1996.

While his party had gone down in flames, in a political world ruled by money Thaksin was uniquely primed for a comeback. Thaksin's companies, after all, had escaped the brunt of the economic crisis. Not only did his businesses recover quickly; most emerged from the crisis stronger than before thanks to the decimation of much of the competition. Even here, it was alleged, Thaksin benefited from his position in the government by receiving advance warning of the upcoming devaluation of the baht.

The economic crisis offered Thaksin the opportunity to deploy his limitless financial means to build a party that would ostensibly better protect Thailand in a globalized economy, offer an alternative to the grey bureaucrats and "professional politicians" who had ruled the country much too long, and finally transform Thai politics by rendering it more hopeful, creative, cooperative, and clean. The customary banalities spouted by every dark horse politician the world over were spruced up with some business school lingo; they were supplemented by the almost comically naïve promise to "bring happiness to the majority of the country." In July 1998, Thaksin was joined by a small group of intellectuals and government officials for the launch of a new political party named *Thai Rak Thai* (literally, "Thais Love Thais"). But the warmth and fuzziness of Thaksin's initial public pronouncements stood in sharp contrast to the aggressiveness of his campaign for electoral support, the cold efficiency with which he set on crafting a winning message, and the combativeness with which he went after opponents. At first, Thai Rak Thai courted big business leaders who had taken a beating in 1997 and sought a bigger role in politics. Then, Thaksin pandered to small business owners and the rural poor by portraying himself as a self-made man and a decisive leader who could protect Thailand's economy without neglecting the workers and entrepreneurs that Chuan and the IMF were supposedly selling out to foreign interests.

At the same time, the crisis presented the budding Thai Rak Thai — initially devoid of but the faintest programmatic pretense — with an obvious narrative in which a group of self-described "outsiders," however well-heeled, could ground their epic quest to challenge the establishment. Thaksin himself noted that he applied "scientific thinking" to engineer the rise of Thai Rak Thai, enlisting consultancy firms and polling organizations to craft a compelling message. The result was what Pasuk and Baker characterize as a "new nationalism" that vowed to defend Thailand from foreign dominance and emphasized the need for the country to integrate into the global economy on its own terms.[26] An economic recovery plan centered on government assistance to small and medium-sized enterprises was announced in 2000. Then, Thaksin rode the wave of discontent in the provinces by putting together a rural platform that could appeal to upcountry voters, leaders, and social movements like the increasingly vocal Assembly of the Poor. The cornerstones of his rural program were an agrarian debt moratorium, the establishment of a million-baht fund for every village, and a thirty baht per visit health care plan. With the endorsement of prominent community organizations came millions of new members and a massive influx of MPs from other parties. At least a hundred of them were bought or cajoled into joining Thai Rak Thai in advance of the 2001 elections.

At the turn of the new millennium, Thailand was hailed as a success story, a shining beacon of freedom in a region where more or less oppressive, corrupt dictatorships are the rule. Things were supposed to be different this time. The country had pulled through the deep financial crisis that enveloped much of Southeast Asia in 1997 without turning to military strongmen or extra-constitutional government. The

---

26. Ibid., pp. 76-80.

generals, for their part, no longer seemed to pose much of a threat — having squandered more political capital than they could ever hope to recover during the massacre of unarmed demonstrators in May 1992. At long last, moreover, a brand new constitution promised to usher in the hitherto elusive consolidation of the country's democratic institutions. And yet, another tragic reversal was just around the corner. Less than fifteen years after residents of Bangkok had chased the military back to the barracks — at the peril and sometimes the expense of their lives — many of the same people now greeted the troops with flowers, cheerfully posing for the cellphone cameras alongside tanks deployed to the capital's major landmarks.

If it once became general, wealth would confer no distinction. It was possible, no doubt, to imagine a society in which wealth, in the sense of personal possessions and luxuries, should be evenly distributed, while power remained in the hands of a small privileged caste. But in practice such a society could not long remain stable. For if leisure and security were enjoyed by all alike, the great mass of human beings who are normally stupefied by poverty would become literate and would learn to think for themselves; and when once they had done this, they would sooner or later realise that the privileged minority had no function, and they would sweep it away. In the long run, a hierarchical society was only possible on the basis of poverty and ignorance.

—GEORGE ORWELL
Nineteen Eighty-Four

TWO

IN NAME OF THE FATHER

> Things were running smoothly until a guy named Thaksin came in. Originally this elite group thought Thaksin would be no different and play by their rules. But Thaksin, being a smartass, had great personal ambition. And he was able to gather enough support and was looking forward more than normal, and the 1997 constitution allowed him to because it was drafted with the purpose of giving the PM a strong hand. He cut off this bridge between the elite and himself. That's why people were pissed off.
>
> —SONDHI LIMTHONGKUL[1]

Whenever Thailand steps close to the brink of military dictatorship, pundits dust off an all-purpose explanation for the chronic instability of the country's democratic institutions. Now as ever, the failure of democracy is said to be rooted in the rift between town and country — in the deep social and cultural cleavage that pits the interests, values, and aspirations of Bangkok's upper-middle classes against those of the urban poor and the uneducated, uncouth provincial masses.

---

[1]. Interview given in 2007. See Shawn Crispin, "Recollections, Revelations of a Protest Leader," *Asia Times Online*, April 27, 2007.

We are told that provincial Thais want something entirely different out of democracy from what the more educated, more value-driven middle-class voters in Bangkok have come to expect. And, on occasion, we are reminded that each group is ready to resort to decidedly undemocratic means to impose its own vision of what "democracy" is all about.

The conventional wisdom tells us that voters in the countryside could not care less about policy or ideology. Most are swayed by their deference to patrons and local authority figures. Most vote not their hearts or minds, but their basest parochial concerns — vulgar banalities like a politician's ability to create jobs, pave roads, build bridges, dig wells, and restore Buddhist temples. And most are eager to sell their votes to the highest bidder. To this day, as many as seven out of every ten of the King's subjects reside in thousands of villages and small towns dotting Thailand's vast rural landscape. As a result, elected legislatures are invariably stacked with representatives whom urban voters despise for their boorishness, incompetence, and overbearing avarice. Inept, predatory administrations, in turn, generate profound disillusionment in Bangkok — triggering a crescendo of support for the kind of military intervention that might once and for all deliver the country from the corruption and moral turpitude of its provincial politicians. The cycle begins anew when the urban middle class awakens to find military rule unpalatable, takes to the streets, suffers the requisite number of casualties, and somehow forces the generals back to the barracks.

This simple narrative recurs with some variation in the foreign scholarship and the Bangkok press, as it does in the work of Thai writers who are openly sympathetic to the plight of provincial voters. It arguably works best as an explanation for democracy's collapse in 1991, its return in 1992, and the bloodshed that marked the intervening period. Academic and activist Anek Laothamatas, in fact, wrote his well known statement on this twisted "tale of two democracies" to explain the build-up to Black May 1992 as well as to identify potential sources of future instability.[2] The story, however, also has considerable bearing on the failure of democracy in 1976. If, in particular, what doomed Thailand's elected government back then was its perceived inability to put up a strong enough fight against the advance of communism, the emergence of a hopelessly fragmented National Assembly reflected the particularism and personalization typical of political competition in the provinces. At the same time, the tacit support that much of the urban electorate offered the coup was grounded in the fear that a fourteen-party government dominated by bungling, money-grubbing politicians would not be capable of shepherding the country through those trying times.

Just as Anek suggested, moreover, the juxtaposition of town and country has figured prominently in the run-up to the 2006 coup and the upheaval that Thailand has experienced since. If deposed Prime Minister Thaksin Shinawatra is especially popular among the urban proletariat and provincial voters in the North and Northeast, his staunchest opposition is found among middle and upper-income voters in the capital city. Provincial voters made Thaksin. With a little help, Bangkokians got rid of him.

Of course, it is hard to deny that important differences in wealth, education, status, consumption habits, and even political culture separate upper-middle-class voters in Bangkok — as Anek defines them, "middle-income persons employed in managerial, executive, or technical positions in the private sector, as well as self-employed professionals such as doctors, nurses, journalists, architects, and lawyers"[3] — from the coolies, peasants, farmers, and petty shopkeepers who populate the country's provinces. And there is little doubt that different kinds of politicians tend to be popular among these broad

---

2. Anek Laothamatas, "A Tale of Two Democracies: Conflicting Perceptions of Elections and Democracy in Thailand," in *The Politics of Elections in Southeast Asia*, ed. Robert H. Taylor (Cambridge University Press, 1996).
3. Ibid., p. 209.

and, lest we forget, internally variegated groups.[4] For precisely these reasons, the conventional wisdom has a strong ring of truth. Its elegant characterization of Thailand's vicious cycle of democracy and dictatorship, cast in the simple terms of a deep social cleavage produced by modernization, renders this highly intelligible narrative ideal for wide dissemination and mass consumption.

But if the chasm between city and countryside is an important reason why Thailand never quite ceased to drift in and out of military dictatorship, the conventional wisdom offers little more than a caricature for the interests and aspirations of both urban and provincial voters. For their part, provincial Thais are not as foolish as those who belittle their loutishness or romanticize their pastoral innocence would have us believe. It should be noted, in this regard, that until very recently provincial voters had never quite been given the option to choose between competing visions of how the country should be governed — and hence put to the test the widely shared notion that their unsophistication would prevent them from making reasoned judgments about national policies and rival campaign platforms. Weak as they have always been because of intermittent repression and internal divisions, political parties never offered much in the way of clear programmatic distinctions that could even faintly appeal to rural voters. Confronted with fast-approaching elections, political parties always took the easy road to victory — relying on the voters' loyalty to local notabilities rather than establishing their own. That provincial Thais do not vote an ideology, then, has less to do with the fact that party platforms would be too difficult to understand or too abstracted from their immediate concerns than the reality that a coherent set of competing ideas has rarely been on offer. The problem is in the supply as much as the demand.

---

4. For instance, see Andrew Walker, "The Rural Constitution and the Everyday Politics of Elections in Northern Thailand," *Journal of Contemporary Asia* 38(2008): 84-105.

Ironically, while former Prime Minister Thaksin Shinawatra is loathed by many in Bangkok on account of his penchant for buying or otherwise rigging elections, his enduring popularity is much less a function of his ability to outbid the competition in the market for votes than it is the consequence of actual policies he implemented. As one of Thailand's richest men, Thaksin had plenty of money to spend and enough ambition to gamble almost all of it away on his political career. But the real game-changer, not to mention his most unforgivable crime, was that Thaksin for the first time "nationalized" elections in the provinces by crafting a simple platform that resonated with voters well beyond the popularity, wealth, and stature of any local candidate. In the wake of the 1997 Asian Crisis, Thaksin effectively combined the old money politics with a program unprecedented for its detail and its focus on long-neglected regions and social classes. Provincial voters rewarded him in spades. Thai Rak Thai won a near-majority in the 2001 elections and a still more commanding mandate in 2005. As expected, when Thailand re-emerged from military rule in late 2007, the same voters handed the People Power Party — the first re-incarnation of the now dissolved TRT — another decisive victory at the ballot box.

At the same time, provincial Thais can hardly be mistaken for paragons of democratic virtue. Lest we forget, it is their support that enabled Thaksin to make of kidnapping, torture, and murder semi-official state policy. To be sure, at the height of his power Thaksin was different things to different people. Some voters probably believed his government's half-hearted denials of any involvement in the extra-judicial killings and the muzzling of the media. Others, who no doubt understood quite well what the government was doing, might simply have taken the good with the bad — having deemed Thaksin's authoritarian bent the acceptable cost of his populist platform. But to many among Thaksin's supporters, the government's heavy-handedness in dealing with protesters, journalists, drug dealers, and presumed insurgents was simply an extension of his leadership and management style. As such, these policies were widely applauded. The War on Drugs was found to have the backing of as much as ninety percent of the Thai electorate. And his suicidal approach to counterinsurgency sparked a wave of nationalist fervor that, at least initially, strengthened Thaksin against his critics in the legislature, the Privy Council, civil society, and the media.[5]

The overwhelming public support that Thaksin's most anti-democratic policies enjoyed can only be understood with reference to the context in which his ascent took place. In the midst of a devastating economic crisis, the Chuan government was seen as weak and indecisive, paralyzed by internal dissension and subservient to foreign interests. Splintered, factionalized, and porous as they were, the existing political parties presented no alternative to get Thailand out of its rut. As least as much as his ideas, it was Thaksin's biography, his projection of strength and decisiveness, and his brash, in-your-face style that offered something really new. Power-hungry politicians with no mission in politics but their own enrichment and little to show for their work but an endless cycle of defections, re-shuffles, and no-confidence motions seemed incapable of confronting the serious challenges the country was facing. Thaksin promised to do so; the aggressiveness with which he subsequently rammed his agenda through what had once been a fractious, do-nothing legislature demonstrated he damn well could.

If the economic crisis had given rise to a wave of "chauvinist resentment"[6] that Thai Rak Thai's brand of nationalism appropriated and then further inflamed, it was in his self-appointed role as the country's strenuous defender from a host of malevolent outsiders that Thaksin successfully recast his

---

5. Duncan McCargo, *Rethinking Thailand's Southern Violence* (Singapore: NUS Press, 2007), pp. 56-61.
6. Maurizio Peleggi, *Thailand: The Worldly Kingdom* (London: Reaktion Books, 2007), p. 127.

opponents as the country's enemies. It was thus that his critics in the media and civil society were accused of "damaging the country."[7] It was thus that everyone killed during the orgy of violence of the War on Drugs was branded "scum" and a "threat to society," that anyone investigating the killings was slandered as being on the drug cartels' payroll, and that every individual or organization who condemned the administration was labeled a menace to Thailand's independence.[8] It was thus that the southern youths who were massacred by the army and police came to be referred to as "beasts."[9] It was thus, at the end of the day, that democracy died in Thailand. By and large, provincial voters enthusiastically approved.

Much like the boors upcountry, the Bangkok middle classes could be said to be neither as high-minded nor quite as effete as the alternative spins to the same conventional wisdom suggest. For all their sophistication, they have shown themselves eager to embrace, unreservedly, a barrage of royalist propaganda extolling the unfailing virtue of questionable characters whose accomplishments are decidedly thin, beyond the spiritualization of their own power. All their democratic values and good-government ideals, moreover, never quite prevented Bangkokians from acquiescing to corrupt, repressive regimes — notwithstanding the occasional bursts of mass indignation that punctuated Thailand's long spells under military rule.

Beyond the apparent lifestyle differences, then, the rift between town and country is arguably about identity and self-image — or its mirror, the long held stereotype that portrays Northeasterners as lazy, halfwitted grunts — more than it is about any coherent ideology or vision of what "democracy" is all about. Incidentally, more or less affluent voters in Bangkok are not the only ones who have proven susceptible to political discourse appealing to a sense of moral superiority. In the

---

7. Pasuk and Baker, *Thaksin*, p. 157.
8. Ibid., p. 164.
9. McCargo, *Rethinking Thailand's Southern Violence*, p. 66.

relatively prosperous South, for instance, the Democrat Party routinely makes reference to the "beautiful political culture" that ostensibly sets the region's principled, incorruptible inhabitants apart from the sycophantic lumpenproletariat to the north and the northeast.[10]

Vast differences in education, wealth, and status notwithstanding, while provincial voters are often said to be easy prey to the machinations of unsavory local bosses, the urban middle class is every bit the pawn of the Bangkok establishment. Once again, Anek is quite right that the millions-strong urban mass of professionals and white-collar workers is the key swing constituency in Thailand's perpetual oscillation between democracy and dictatorship. Depending on the circumstances, their active participation or tacit support is, indeed, required to bring down an elected government through extra-constitutional means. But the initiative to build up a critical mass of disgust for the elected leadership does not originate from lawyers and doctors — much less the trifling office worker in the polyester slacks and $5 shirt.

For one thing, the mainstream press is understandably less reluctant to report on the corruption of provincial politicians than it is to investigate the indiscretions of the palace, the military, and its corporate owners. More importantly, the demonstrations and prolonged sit-ins designed to raise awareness of the government's mendacity, greed, and treasonous impulses can only be mobilized with the resources of urban elites — Bangkok's business community, its pompous coterie of "minor" princes and princesses, and a vast palace-controlled network of high-ranking officials in both the civilian and military bureaucracy.[11]

A case in point is the so-called People's Alliance for De-

---

10. See Marc Askew, *Performing Political Identity: The Democrat Party in Southern Thailand* (Chiang Mai: Silkworm Books, 2008), p. 17.
11. For a summary, see Duncan McCargo, "Thai Politics as Reality TV," *The Journal of Asian Studies* 68(2009): 7-19.

mocracy (PAD) — the most vocal, best organized opposition to Thaksin and his surrogates. In truth, it is hard to decide whether the PAD is less about "democracy" or "the people," for whom it has consistently exhibited little more than paternalistic condescension. It is certainly an alliance, though, or better yet, the bastard child of a long, unholy marriage of privileged constituencies. For the rich, the generals, and the noble, the idea of elected government is acceptable so long as such governments are weak, fragmented, and unprincipled enough to be easily manipulated, bought off, or otherwise kept in check. Whenever the influence of these constituencies is on the wane, however, the drumbeat for military intervention invariably sounds in the distance. If the case can be made with a straight face, they will invoke the need to restore "true" democracy — to pry the reins of government away from the hands of corrupt politicians. If that argument is no longer serviceable, they will abandon all pretense of liberal propriety and argue that Thailand cannot afford democracy — not so long as the majority of its citizens remain bumbling imbeciles eager to sell their votes to all manners of murderers and thieves.

Formed in February 2006, at first the PAD grounded its crusade to remove Thaksin's elected administration in the least controversial of these claims — the need to re-establish the kind of "real democracy" that Thaksin's populism, corruption, and taste for human rights abuses all but foreclosed. Whatever the thousands of ordinary people who attended its rallies might have thought, however, one need not dig too deep into its background, rhetoric, and operational strategy to realize just how hostile the PAD really is to the idea of democracy — that which this "people's alliance" is supposedly "for." Especially illustrative in this regard are the stories of PAD leaders Chamlong Srimuang and Sondhi Limthongkul, both compelling profiles in carpetbagging and *trasformismo*.

Known for his ostentatious adherence to Buddhist precepts, retired Major-General Chamlong Srimuang is the face of the 1992 democratic uprising. In the intervening time, Chamlong had retired from politics after driving his old party — *Palang Dharma*, or "Moral Force" — into the ground as a result of the uproar caused by Thaksin's recruitment. Having supported Thaksin in the 2001 elections and publicly defended him when he first came under fire in 2002,[12] it was only in 2004 that Chamlong finally awoke to the fact that Thaksin had an authoritarian streak and was neck deep in "money politics"[13] — something that anyone in his own party, particularly those who left in protest after he elevated Thaksin to a position of leadership, could have told him a decade earlier. But while Thaksin had not much changed since the mid-1990s, by then the mood of Bangkok's upper crust was certainly turning. Chamlong, whose popularity never transcended Bangkok's city limits, was no doubt painfully aware that he had stained his own legacy by introducing Thaksin to politics. It is to his patrons and supporters in Bangkok that he publicly apologized in 2004, insisting that he now deeply regretted having brought upon them the scourge of Thaksin Shinawatra.

Sondhi Limthongkul is a leading member of Bangkok's moneyed elites — one of the first groups to break faith with Thaksin. Having built a large, international media holding company in the 1980s, like his nemesis Sondhi spent much of the 1990s expanding his reach into the growing markets for mobile phones and satellite television. Unlike Thaksin, however, his businesses foundered in the 1997 Asian Crisis, leaving Sondhi bankrupt and under official investigation. As most of Bangkok's business community did at the time, Sondhi initially supported Thaksin wholeheartedly. After the 2001 elections, one his publications famously called Thaksin's government "the best the country has ever had." By 2004,

---

12. "Chamlong Defends Thaksin's Attitude," *The Nation*, March 28, 2002.
13. "Former Mentor: Thaksin Was My Mistake," *The Nation*, August 23, 2004.

however, Sondhi had fallen out with the Prime Minister. The relationship had soured over the previous two years, owing to Thaksin's refusal to grant Sondhi the television station he demanded.[14] It did not help matters that Thaksin failed to intervene in defense of Sondhi's embattled associate Viroj Nualkhair — who, as CEO of Krung Thai Bank, had forgiven billions of Sondhi's debts.[15] Sondhi definitively turned on his old friend after the administration yanked his Channel 9 talk show "Thailand Weekly" off the air.

Quite aside from the personal animosity that some of them might have harbored, however, most offensive to Sondhi's ilk was Thaksin's economic policy. For Bangkok's business elites, it was never about the extra-judicial killings, the corruption, the vote-buying, or the intimidation of the press — transgressions they have no difficulty excusing if committed by governments sympathetic to their interests. The real issue was "Thaksinomics." Once again, on this matter the PAD had a decent case to make. There is no question, in particular, that Thaksin's policies reflected his determination to build a more efficient and expansive network of patronage — one that would maximize his own power by going over the heads of provincial bosses — more than to promote rural development. There is little doubt that the village loan funds were doled out selectively by local politicians to further their own interests, while monitoring mechanisms verifying that the loans would be destined to investment and not private consumption were weak or non-existent. And it is beyond dispute that Thaksin employed dubious accounting practices to keep track of public expenditures on those very programs.

But that is not the point. Sondhi and his friends regularly have recourse to their own political connections to get cash, contracts, and concessions from the government on the tax-

---

14. McCargo, "Thai Politics as Reality TV," p. 8.
15. "The Good Old Days," *The Nation*, November 30, 2005. See also "The Truth About Thaksin, Sondhi," *The Nation*, November 29, 2005.

payer's dime. Indeed, that is precisely how some of them, Thaksin included, got rich in the first place. After all, it was only thanks to incestuous, corrupt deals that a few dozen, mostly Sino-Thai business families — the lifeblood of the PAD — concentrated such an astounding amount of wealth in the hands of so few people. At least since the late 1930s, wealthy families have shared their largesse with big men in the military and civilian bureaucracy, appointing them to spectacularly lucrative positions on their companies' boards of directors and funneling money to state-sponsored or privately owned firms controlled by generals.[16] In return, they got favorable legislation, tax breaks, government contracts, protection from competition, and much sought-after concessions that allowed them to turn most sectors of Thailand's economy into monopolies or oligopolies.[17]

Suffice it to say that on the eve of the Asian Crisis, the combined revenues of Thailand's top two hundred companies, most of which remained family-owned or family-controlled, amounted to sixty-two percent of GDP; that of the top thirty companies, almost forty percent of GDP.[18] Among many others, the PAD could now count on the generous financial backing of families leading Thailand's four largest private conglomerates[19] — Bangkok Bank, Kasikorn Bank, Charoen Pokphand, and Thai Charoen Corporation. For much of 2008, big business bankrolled the PAD's operations to the tune of at least a million baht per day.[20]

The filthy rich, of course, were only too happy to go along with Thaksin when his campaign looked to keep them aboard

---

16. Suehiro Akira, *Capital Accumulation in Thailand, 1855-1985* (Chiang Mai: Silkworm Books, 1996), p. 170.
17. Ibid., p. 232.
18. Natenapha Wailerdsak, "Companies in Crisis," in *Thai Capital after the 1997 Crisis*, ed. Pasuk Phongpaichit and Chris Baker (Chiang Mai: Silkworm Books, 2008), p. 40.
19. Ibid., p. 39. These figures refer to the year 2000.
20. Patrick Winn, "Thailand's Costly Protests: Who's Footing the Bill?," *Huffington Post*, December 11, 2008.

a veritable gravy train of pecuniary and regulatory benefits. In the run-up to the 2001 elections, Thai Rak Thai had made a strong effort to court Bangkok's battered business community, who vociferously bemoaned having been "sold out" by politicians during the Asian Crisis. His predecessors, Chuan and Chavalit, had come under withering criticism for letting business owners down. At the time, it was widely expected that Thaksin — a Bangkok politician with virtually no street cred in the provinces — would take care of his own people first, offering business leaders greater protection and privileged access to the policymaking process. Their hopes, however, were quickly disappointed as both prongs of Thaksin's "dual track" economic philosophy appeared to benefit constituencies other than their own.

On the one hand, Thaksin harnessed the machinery of government to maximize the competitive edge that his own businesses — as well as those of relatives and cronies — already enjoyed over much of the competition. Given the breadth of Shin Corp and its satellite businesses, his administration posed a serious threat to the interests of much of Bangkok's business elite.[21] In addition, Thaksin's promotion of trade and foreign direct investment threatened the dominance that a few dozen Sino-Thai families had enjoyed since the late 1950s over commercial banking, agribusiness, and most manufacturing. Many of these "client capitalist" families had suffered mightily from the Asian Crisis — deeply in debt, they had been forced to rely on massive foreign investments in their firms to stay afloat.[22] Further exposure to foreign competition was therefore anathema to domestic oligopolists accustomed to buying, for relatively cheap, the state's mercantilist protections.[23]

---

21. See Pasuk and Baker, *Thaksin*, p. 229.
22. Natenapha, "Companies in Crisis".
23. See Jaimie Seaton and George Wehrfritz, "All Politics Isn't Local: The Real Enemy of Demonstrators Threatening to Shut Down the Country is Globalization," *Newsweek*, September 6, 2008.

On the other hand, electoral calculations based on little more than a simple head count quickly shifted the focus of "Thaksinomics" from big business in the city to mom-and-pop rural operations. At least since the late 1950s, rural voters have reliably served as the backdrop for photo-ops designed to demonstrate the greatness and merit of Bangkok's biggest men — His Majesty the King foremost among them. But they never really earned the right to share in the country's economic prosperity — not lest the subversion of natural hierarchies of wealth, status, and power hasten the destruction of Thai culture and society. Among what the *Bangkok Post* felicitously named, for once, the "blue blood jet set" of the nation's capital, any love for Thaksin was bound to be short-lived.

Among the myriad charges the PAD leveled against Thaksin, the one that truly stuck was that the former Prime Minister was hell-bent on "selling the country off" — determined to auction Thailand's soul away to the highest (foreign) bidders, presumably in exchange for money he could use to feed his electoral machine and quench his insatiable greed. In this respect, the PAD made the most out of the January 2006 sale of Shin Corp to Temasek Holdings, Singapore's sovereign fund. To the PAD's great benefit, the transaction soon proved highly controversial. In a stunning display of arrogance, greed, and stupidity, the Shinawatras found a way to avoid paying capital gains taxes on the $2 billion sale, inflaming the anger that had been simmering in Bangkok against the family's alleged use of public office for gargantuan private gain. Equally important, because the sale included highly sensitive assets, Thaksin was faulted for his disregard of Thailand's economic integrity as well as his reckless endangerment of the country's national security.

Even as it was agitating for a better, more complete version of democracy — one supposedly not limited to the few seconds it takes to mark a ballot and drop it into a box — the PAD's behavior belied the loftiness of its stated objectives. In and of itself, pleading with the military and the King to step in was not terribly suspicious. The PAD had a point in arguing that undemocratic means may be required to remove anti-democratic governments. After all, the world is replete with dictators who derive a shallow legitimacy from elections that the opposition has no real chance of winning. And tyranny of the majority is still tyranny. It is rather the PAD's virulent, xenophobic brand of nationalism and perhaps especially its fanatical royalism that should have raised eyebrows. Given the monarchy's enormous prestige, to identify the movement with the defense of His Majesty the King was perhaps the most effective way to soften the Prime Minister's support — or at least earn the PAD a measure of acceptance among the masses of urban middle-class voters, whose acquiescence was required to precipitate Thaksin's ouster. But the PAD's constant manufacturing of far-fetched conspiracies, its habit of accusing its critics of treason and *lèse majesté*, and its repeated calls to "restore" unspecified "powers" of which the King has allegedly been deprived — never mind that the royal family was arguably more wealthy, powerful, and widely revered in the mid-2000s than at any point in the history of the Chakri dynasty — sure smacked of an odd way to work for democracy.

Incidentally, the PAD's actions would have presented a dilemma to anyone whose power depends on the monarchy's image. If, on the one hand, the PAD was an effective thorn in the side of Thaksin and his allies, on the other hand its naked opportunism and the transparently unprincipled, disreputable characters at its helm threatened to cheapen royal symbolism and diminish the monarchy's prestige. Establishment figures like Surayud Chulanont repeatedly warned Sondhi to desist, as his calls for royal intervention intensified in late 2005. Later, Sondhi was charged with *lèse majesté* after publicly repeating invectives leveled at the royal family by a Thaksin supporter, while the King himself seems to have confessed to palace insiders his contempt for the PAD.[24] When Sondhi survived an assassination attempt, in April 2009, one might be forgiven for suspecting that putting a hundred or so bullets through his windshield was somebody's way of suggesting that he had outlived his purpose. Sondhi himself accused prominent aristocrats and army brass of ordering the hit. He attributed the attempt on his life to the efforts of a "powerful man" intent on sending a "powerful message" — his unusual reticence to name names pointing in the direction of someone with unmentionable connections.[25]

Be that as it may, the PAD's initial "democratic" platform won it the backing of many ordinary people in Bangkok as well as a number of civil society organizations who had once supported Thaksin's rise. Large anti-government demonstrations were staged in the capital in February 2006. Whether by accident or by design, the show of force seems to have driven the Prime Minister to give in to his major weaknesses — his impulsiveness and pride. Thaksin, who had taken three quarters of the seats awarded in legislative elections held just a year earlier, walked right into the trap laid by those who publicly claimed he had lost his legitimacy. He dissolved the House of Representatives and scheduled new elections for April, challenging his sworn enemies to come up with some hard evidence that the people had lost trust in his leadership.

Predictably, Thai Rak Thai would win the elections in a landslide, outdistancing its rivals by millions of votes — the kind of margin that would make the tens of thousands of people his opponents had brought out to the streets of Bangkok seem paltry by comparison. Knowing very well they stood no chance of denting Thaksin's electoral dominance, all opposition parties boycotted the contest. Despite Thai Rak Thai's

---

24. See US Embassy Bangkok, "Palace Insider Tells Ambassador of the King's Opposition to a Coup and to PAD Protests," *Diplomatic Cable 08BANGKOK3317*, November 9, 2008.
25. "'Powerful Man Wants to Send Powerful Message:' Sondhi," *The Nation*, May 4, 2009.

success, the PAD caught a major break when about a third of the voters who bothered to show up cast a ballot rejecting all candidates. Shortly thereafter, His Majesty the King gave a famous speech to a batch of newly appointed judges in which he urged the judiciary to "solve" the country's current "problem" and reminded them of their oath to "work for democracy." He then asked a rhetorical question: "Should the elections be nullified?" His Majesty would not say, but noted that at least in his opinion the conduct of the election had been "undemocratic." Right on cue, the Constitutional Court voided the election two weeks later, on suspect legal grounds. Before Thaksin could sweep a new round of voting, the army moved in and seized power. The PAD formally disbanded and virtually disappeared from the scene.

After just over a year in power, the military beat a rather bashful retreat to the barracks, roundly ridiculed for the glacial speed with which the old men appointed by the junta had gone about conducting the nation's business. With the December 2007 elections, it became apparent that the generals had accomplished little. To be sure, Thaksin had been removed and subjected to a number of judicial probes. But even though his immediate re-entry into politics appeared unlikely, Thaksin made a triumphant return to Thailand under the auspices of a sympathetic government led by new Prime Minister Samak Sundaravej.

The choice of Samak would prove to be one of most damaging mistakes Thaksin ever made. Aside from being a veteran Bangkok politician with no currency in the provinces and few of the personal qualities that made Thaksin a folk hero among the underprivileged, Samak had made his name as an ultra-conservative, having previously shilled for the military and the palace by playing an active role in support of the brutal crackdowns of 1976 and 1992. Samak's historical ties with the military and the monarchy, however, earned the new government no sympathy from generals and palace insiders, determined as they were to destroy Thaksin and his proxies whoever they might be. At the same time, Samak's disturbing record gave the resurgent PAD a chance to portray its campaign as the continuation of the struggle for democracy that had famously claimed the lives of hundreds of people in 1973, 1976, and 1992.

Given Chamlong Srimuang's leadership role and the involvement of several former student leaders from the 1970s, the PAD did have an element of continuity with past democratic movements. But the reality is that the democratic movements of times past never enjoyed the kind of protection that institutions like the military and the palace afforded the PAD. Nor did they ever receive much in the way of financial backing from Bangkok's feudal, military, and capitalist elites. These constituencies, whose long-standing dominance over Thai politics and society is threatened by the possibility that Thailand might embark upon a path to real democratization, have rather more commonly sought to crush democratic challenges to their rule.

While, moreover, many among the former student leaders have long since soured on the idea of liberal democracy,[26] it should be recalled that Chamlong has not been as fervent or as consistent an advocate of "democracy" as his supporters would have it. In 1976, Chamlong was among the leaders of a group of military officers who supported the repression of Thammasat University students as well as the military coup that ensued. Though Chamlong's role in the incident remains unclear, it is well known that the "Young Turks" actively undermined the democratic governments of the mid-1970s, which they regarded as a threat to the nation at a time when Southeast Asian countries seemed to fall like dominos to a series of communist insurgencies.

Indeed, the PAD's ideology and worldview are rather more sinisterly reminiscent of royalist vigilante groups like the Vil-

---

26. See, for instance, Thongchai Winichakul, "Nationalism and the Radical Intelligentsia in Thailand," *Third World Quarterly* 29(2008): 575-591, p. 575.

lage Scouts and the Red Gaurs[27] most famous for carrying out the 1976 massacre at Thammasat University. But since the events of 1976, which do not quite square with the country's official ideology, are typically discussed only in the broadest generalities,[28] it was not difficult for the PAD to blast Samak for his involvement (and his continuing denials that significant loss of life had occurred) without raising difficult questions about the responsibilities borne by the palace, palace associates, and palace idolaters.

Still, the failure of the military-led restoration of "democracy" to prevent the return to power of forces loyal to Thaksin constituted something of a problem for the PAD. The new government, in fact, had come to power through elections organized and overseen by the junta — which had tried its damnedest to secure a victory for the Democrat Party — under rules designed by a military-appointed Constitution Drafting Assembly that included prominent PAD sympathizers and supporters. Moreover, while the PAD could well accuse key government figures like Samak and Interior Minister Chalerm Yubumrung of being loathsome in their own right, the politicians who had won seats under the banner of the People Power Party were those who had survived the ban from politics handed down concurrently with the dissolution of Thai Rak Thai in May 2007.

It is at this point that the PAD abandoned all pretense of fighting for "democracy." In July 2008, its leaders advanced their boldest, most sweeping proposal yet — the "New Poli-

---

27. See, for instance, Katherine A. Bowie, *Rituals of National Loyalty: An Anthropology of the State and the Village Scout Movement in Thailand* (New York: Columbia University Press, 1997).
28. The largely unsuccessful attempt to earn official recognition for the victims of 1976 is detailed in Klima, *The Funeral Casino*, p. 170, and Thongchai Winichakul, "Remembering/Silencing the Traumatic Past: The Ambivalence Narratives of the October 6, 1976 Massacre in Bangkok," in *Cultural Crisis and Social Memory: Modernity and Identity in Thailand and Laos*, ed. Charles F. Keyes and Shigeharu Tanabe (London: Routledge/Curzon, 2002), 243-283.

tics." Sondhi Limthongkul now took to arguing that democracy was useless in Thailand, where most voters lack the "intelligence and wisdom" to know what to do with their political rights.[29] Sondhi's words reflected what has long been a widely shared belief in Bangkok. In the wake of the coup, National Legislative Assembly President Meechai Ruchuphan famously compared ruling the bovine people of Thailand with a democratic constitution to using a Rolls-Royce to plow a paddy field.[30]

In point of fact, the New Politics is but a hodgepodge of reactionary proposals designed to roll back much of the freedom the Thai people have achieved over the past eight decades. Perhaps the most controversial among its propositions called for the establishment of a legislature composed of seventy percent appointed members — something reminiscent of the system of "tutelary democracy" Thailand lived under for much of the 1930s, 1940s, and 1950s, when the bureaucracy and the military reserved the right to rule with minimal interference from elected representatives until the day the Thai masses would prove "ready" for democracy. The suggestion, moreover, that the military be legally allowed to take over the reins of government whenever a civilian administration is judged incompetent or corrupt, fails to act upon *lèse majesté* allegations, or is perceived to have jeopardized the country's sovereignty — in other words, when it runs afoul of the PAD's agenda — sounded much like an attempt to give legal sanction to the kind of praetorianism Thailand experienced for the better part of the twentieth century. Meanwhile, to suggest that even greater formal powers should vested in the King is to signal that Thailand's problems are best addressed by rolling the clock all the way back to 1932.

It should be noted that the use of the word "democracy"

---

29. Jaimie Seaton and George Wehrfritz, "Crackdown," *Newsweek*, September 2, 2008.
30. "Blame People, Not the 1997 Charter," *The Nation*, October 29, 2006.

in the title of an organization devoted to the disenfranchisement of tens of millions of people should not be mistaken for mere chutzpah or hypocrisy. Nor is it just a definitional question about the appropriate size of the *demos*. To claim the mantle of true democrats while denouncing democracy as a dangerous utopia is rather reflective of a far more insidious worldview. In 1932, none other than Benito Mussolini wrote these words in his "Doctrine of Fascism:"

> Fascism is opposed to Democracy, which equates the nation to the majority, lowering it to the level of that majority; nevertheless it is the purest form of democracy if the nation is conceived, as it should be, qualitatively and not quantitatively.[31]

In ideological terms, it is thus that the PAD can claim to embody "the will of the people" even though its entire agenda is predicated upon replacing the people's choices with their own. The natural order made it their role to think *for* the masses. The PAD's, in fact, is possibly a superior form of democracy — one that recognizes the functions proper to each of the various components of Thailand's social organism. Those who oppose the PAD's vision, in this sense, are "traitors" and "enemies of the nation" because a society of equals undermines natural hierarchies whose preservation is integral to the survival of the organism as a whole. For the PAD, what the majority actually thinks is irrelevant. The "will of the people" is what they say it is. It is simply not within the purview of the uncouth peasant, the ignorant drudge, or the feckless cab driver to hold political opinions.

The launch of the New Politics coincided with the adoption of an increasingly confrontational, violent approach. After reviving the decades-old dispute over the Preah Vihear temple complex, in an attempt to inflame racial hatred and spark an armed confrontation with Cambodia, the PAD

---

31. Benito Mussolini, *The Doctrine of Fascism* (New York: Howard Fertig, 2006[1932]).

stepped up the sparsely attended, slumbering sit-in that its members had been staging on Rachadamnoen Avenue since the last week of May 2008. Conscious that, in Thailand, there is no catalyst for change more powerful than death,[32] PAD leaders regularly attempted to bait the police into using force to disperse the crowds.[33] Time and time again, the nation held its collective breath as the PAD announced to the press that the inevitable violent crackdown was imminent. In late August, thousands of PAD supporters — some of them armed with guns, sticks, knives, and small explosives — occupied the Government House, laid waste to key Ministries, stormed the offices of the National Broadcasting Services of Thailand (NBT), and temporarily shut down airports in the southern cities of Phuket, Hat Yai, and Krabi. Prime Minister Samak Sundaravej stepped back, refusing to give the military the pretext for intervening or hand the PAD a bloody shirt its leaders could wave around Bangkok.

The PAD finally got its blood on October 7, when skirmishes outside the National Assembly left at least two people dead and scores injured. By that time, Thailand had a new Prime Minister, Thaksin's brother-in-law Somchai Wongsawat — Samak having been forced to resign a month earlier by a Constitutional Court decision that ruled his role as the host of a weekend cooking show illegal. To the surprise of many, the violence on October 7 did not precipitate the coup the PAD had been clamoring for — the familiar kind of coup featuring the deployment of tanks, the proscription of political organizations, and the imposition of martial law. The PAD, in fact, got something much better than that: the

---
32. For an account of the significance, indeed the necessity of death to political change in Thailand, see Klima, *The Funeral Casino*.
33. Recently leaked diplomatic cables cite a palace insider reporting that the PAD was aiming for the death of at least two dozen of its supporters to bring down the government. See US Embassy Bangkok, "Palace Insider Tells Ambassador of the King's Opposition to a Coup and to PAD Protests," *Diplomatic Cable 08BANGKOK3317*, November 9, 2008.

slow but inexorable cooking of the government's goose. At the end of the day, that would amount to a coup all the same, but the pretense of legality was carefully preserved through the outward observance of otherwise worthless constitutional provisions and parliamentary procedures.

The siege of the National Assembly would turn out to have inflicted a fatal blow on the new government. As if the humiliation of having lost control of the Government House weeks earlier had not been enough, widely circulated images of members of parliament clambering up the walls separating the National Assembly from the Vimanmek Mansion to escape the wrath of protesters were a devastating sign that the administration had lost its ability to govern. Worse still, the rich symbolism of panic-stricken democratic representatives seeking refuge in a former royal residence recently converted into a museum commemorating the reign of King Chulalongkorn, the founder of Thai royal absolutism, seemed to portend yet another historical regression in the face of democracy's apparent failure to provide the country with a functional government.

Never mind the circumstances in which it took place — during the day, scores of policemen were injured by PAD guards who repeatedly fired guns, hurled ping-pong bombs, and even drove a bus into police lines — the violence also prompted key figures in the Thai establishment to openly state their support for the PAD. Democrat Party leader Abhisit Vejjajiva joined former Prime Minister Anand Panyarachun at the funeral of Police Lieutenant Colonel Methee Chatmontri — a PAD cadre who had died on October 7. Methee had blown up on the bomb he had himself driven to the offices of Chat Thai, a junior coalition partner of the ruling People Power Party. Meanwhile, Her Majesty the Queen pledged large donations for hospitals treating PAD supporters injured in the fighting. With her daughter Princess Chulabhorn at her side, she attended the funeral of Angkana Radabpanyawoot, a young woman killed outside the parliament building

— to this day, it remains unclear whether she was hit in the chest by a tear gas canister the police had fired, or whether she was killed by the accidental blast of an explosive device she (or others around her) might have been carrying. Within days, army Commander-in-Chief Anupong Paochinda went on television to declare that the government should take responsibility and resign.[34]

Equally important was the cover that the events of October 7 gave the PAD to escalate its activities. Shortly thereafter, Sondhi announced that the PAD was renouncing nonviolence. Evidently, it was in Gandhi's writings that the PAD had found the inspiration to gun down policemen. On November 25, thousands of PAD supporters spearheaded by the customary militia of strung-out ruffians stormed Thailand's two major international airports — Suvarnabhumi and Don Muang. But while forcing the closure of the airports, stranding thousands of travelers, once there the PAD behaved much differently than it had after seizing temporary control of government buildings. This time, the airport's premises were not trashed or ransacked. Curiously, considering that the owners of King Power International — the company holding a monopoly concession to operate all duty-free shops at Suvarnabhumi — had long been associated with Thaksin loyalist Newin Chidchob, the PAD sealed off the stores and put them under twenty-four-hour guard.[35]

The government reacted by declaring the state of emergency, but Anupong predictably refused to enforce it. Evidently skeptical of the protection the army proffered, the Prime Minister temporarily moved the seat of government to the city of Chiang Mai, deep into Thaksin country, flanked by a more dependable police escort. With every passing day, the prospect of re-taking the airports by force looked certain to

---

34. "Coup via TV?," *The Nation*, October 17, 2008.
35. See Dan Rivers' CNN report from the airport terminal on November 28, 2008: http://edition.cnn.com/2008/WORLD/asiapcf/11/28/thailand.airport.protests/.

end in a bloodbath and massive property damage. The PAD was not only heavily armed and continuously re-stocked — its gun-toting auxiliary forces having successfully broken through police roadblocks on the way to the airport. It was now abundantly clear that its leaders were confident enough in their own righteousness to have little reservation about sending men, women and children to their deaths in the service of the noble cause — restoring Thailand to its filthy rich, rightful owners. Somchai's reluctance to send in poorly trained police units to break up the illegal occupation was understandable. Suvarnabhumi International Airport would have looked like the most grotesque of butcher shops had the police carried out the dispersal operations.

The stage was now set for the royalist establishment to drive the final stake into the heart of the government. After all, as the standoff continued to deface Thailand's international image and inflict incalculable damage upon the Thai economy, the government had amply demonstrated that it was of no use whatsoever to the country, having failed to accomplish anything of significance. It was in this context of protracted stalemate that, on December 2, the Constitutional Court staged its widely anticipated "judicial coup" — dissolving the ruling People Power Party for relatively trivial infractions committed by one of its executives in the 2007 elections. The Prime Minister resigned. Ever defiant, the PAD announced it would continue its occupations until the entire cabinet had gone.[36] To the surprise of many, however, within hours its leaders reversed themselves, declared victory, and vacated the airports. The PAD, on its own, can run roughshod over Thailand, but it cannot do so with impunity without the backing of powerful people. At long last, someone whose orders the PAD could not afford to ignore had spoken.

---

36. "PAD: Entire Cabinet Must Leave Office," *The Nation* (Online Breaking News), December 2, 2008.

Big Brother is infallible and all-powerful. Every success, every achievement, every victory, every scientific discovery, all knowledge, all wisdom, all happiness, all virtue, are held to issue directly from his leadership and inspiration. Nobody has ever seen Big Brother. He is a face on the hoardings, a voice on the telescreen. We may be reasonable sure that he will never die, and there is already considerable uncertainty as to when he was born. Big Brother is the guise in which the Party chooses to exhibit itself to the world. His function is to act as a focusing point for love, fear, and reverence, which are more easily felt towards an individual than towards an organization.

—GEORGE ORWELL
Nineteen Eighty-Four

THREE

TYRANNY OF THE BIG MEN

> In truth, the problem is not that upcountry voters don't know how to use their vote, and that the result is distorted by patronage and vote-buying. The problem is that they have learnt to use the vote only too well.
>
> —Chang Noi[1]

Thailand's 2007 constitution begins with a tawdry, obscene fabrication. With Orwellian audacity, its preamble states that "Thailand has been under the rule of democratic government with the King as head of state for more than seventy-five years." No mention is made of aborted transitions and military takeovers. No importance is given to the decades of repression Thailand experienced under the thumb of ghastly military dictators — men who governed the country with a level of savagery only exceeded by their greed. No role is attributed to the hundreds of brave young Thais who died in the mass protests of 1973 and 1992, just so that others would have a say on how they should live. Not so much as a footnote is reserved for the students at Thammasat University, whom paramilitary death squads raped, murdered, and hanged from

---

1. Chang Noi (pseudonym), "The Facts About Vote-Buying and Patronage," *The Nation*, September 1, 2008.

trees — their eyes ripped out of their sockets, their mouths stuffed with old shoes — in October 1976.

The official, comic-book version of Thai history that the government routinely rams down the throats of millions of schoolchildren has no place for the Thai people's painful struggle for democracy. Those who died, lost limbs, went to jail, or fled to the jungle for the cause did all this for no reason whatsoever. They were fighting for what they already had, the fools. The 1932 coup? Not necessary. King Prajadhipok was ready to relinquish his absolute powers, had anyone bothered to ask him politely. The 1973 and 1976 massacres? The students were misguided. And, under the circumstances, Thanom was not all that bad. Black May 1992? Again, it is hard to see why the demonstrators were in such a rush to topple Suchinda. As the His Majesty the King said, the constitution his government wrote was "reasonable." In any event, had the protesters just waited a little while, they could have amended it through the democratic process, which of course has been functioning uninterruptedly for over seventy-five years.

Plenty of elections have been held in Thailand since the 1930s, at a frequency which has at times surpassed that of countries with rather more distinguished democratic records. But many such elections took place under conditions of severely limited competition, had their outcome predetermined by fraud or massive deployment of state resources, or in any case turned out to be irrelevant to the exercise of real political power. For much of the intervening time, moreover, government alternation has been accomplished through coups, not elections, while most of the "permanent" constitutions that have cyclically been promulgated, suspended, and unceremoniously repealed were designed as a way to provide the regime of the day with the veneer of a legal foundation, more than to regulate anything vaguely resembling democratic competition.

Government propaganda notwithstanding, Thailand has only been a "democracy" in any meaningful sense of the word for a relatively small portion of its post-absolutist history. In each such instance, the military had to step in to "restore order" and "protect the unity of the nation."

In light of Thaksin's sickening record, one could be forgiven for having sympathized with the argument made in support of the 2006 coup. The case against Thaksin was at least more cogent than the one cooked up to justify the removal of Chatichai's own "elected dictatorship" in 1991. But we should have known better than to think there is any such thing as a "democratic coup d'état." Certainly, Thailand never experienced one. Thailand, moreover, is a country where human rights abuses — whether perpetrated by the army, the police, or paramilitary death squads — have never been punished. Thanom Kittikachorn got a swell state funeral paid for by His Majesty the King. The Red Gaurs and Village Scouts were never even sought for questioning. Suchinda Kraprayoon was granted blanket amnesty while the bodies of those he murdered were still warm.

Considering that some of the men most commonly associated with the coup do not have a human rights record any more respectable than Thaksin's, there was little indication that things would be different this time. Surayud Chulanont, the Privy Councilor and retired general chosen by the junta to serve as Prime Minister in the wake of the coup, is the same man who led the special forces responsible for well-documented atrocities at the Royal Hotel on May 19, 1992.[2] The coup's mastermind, General Prem Tinsulanonda, cut his teeth in the 1970s by leading a gruesome counterinsurgency campaign against the Communist Party of Thailand in the Northeast — a campaign defined by the same extensive, systematic recourse to extra-judicial executions for which the PAD faulted Thaksin. Prem, incidentally, has the blood of perhaps thousands of Cambodian citizens on his hands. Indeed, it was during his tenure as Prime Minister that Pol

---

2. Thomas Fuller, "Thai Junta Shores Up Role in Politics," *International Herald Tribune*, October 1, 2006.

Pot was given sanctuary on Thai soil. For six years beginning in 1985, Brother Number One lived in a comfortable plantation villa near the border city of Trat, under the protection of Thailand's Special Forces Task Force 838, free to direct the remnants of the Khmer Rouge in the bloody civil war that ravaged western Cambodia.

The War on Drugs itself, perhaps the most shameful chapter in Thaksin's tenure as Prime Minister, was inspired by none other than King Bhumibol, who spoke of such "war" in his 2002 birthday speech. Shortly thereafter, Privy Councilor Phichit Kunlawanit waxed genocidal about the need to execute as many as sixty thousand drug dealers and drug fiends to deliver the nation of any residual "bad karma."[3] And once Thaksin had declared victory, in time for His Majesty's birthday, King Bhumibol publicly endorsed the campaign, noting that "victory in the War on Drugs is good." He went on to say: "They may blame the crackdown for more than 2,500 deaths, but this is a small price to pay. If the Prime Minister failed to curb [the drugs trade], over the years the number of deaths would easily surpass this toll."[4] Given that the number of people murdered in his name over the last six decades is perhaps several times as large, it is not altogether surprising that His Majesty would consider 2,500 human lives "a small price to pay."

When the junta declared it had seized power to right Thaksin's wrongs, then, there were good reasons to be skeptical. Perhaps as a result, the measures taken in the first, heady days after the coup appeared to be aimed at dispelling doubts about the generals' true motives. Shortly after being appointed Prime Minister, Surayud visited the South and extended a tearful apology to family members of the victims of Tak Bai.

---

3. See Michael K. Connors, "Ambivalent about Rights: 'Accidental' Killing Machines, Democracy, and Coups d'Etat," *Southeast Asia Research Centre Working Paper No. 102*, November 2009, p. 8.
4. See, for instance, Daniel Ten Kate, "Thailand to Restart War on Drugs," *Asia Sentinel*, March 4, 2008.

A few months later, the government launched investigations into the human rights abuses committed in the context of the War on Drugs and the southern insurgency.[5] At the same time, the generals impaneled a commission to look into twenty government programs suspected to have been tainted by corruption. The Assets Examination Committee was charged with probing Thaksin's "unusual wealth" as well as specific episodes of tax evasion, corruption, and abuse of power. And the police were instructed to explore the possibility of charging Thaksin with as many as six counts of lèse majesté.

Four years on, it is painfully obvious that the generals never had any intention of seeking justice on behalf of the Thai people. To be sure, Thaksin was hit with a barrage of judicial proceedings — investigations into the Ratchadaphisek land deal, the Exim Bank case, the two- and three-digit lottery case, the sale of Shin Corp, and the shareholder structure of SC Assets Plc. He was convicted, in absentia, and sentenced to two years in prison for his role in the Ratchadaphisek affair.[6] At the same time, Thaksin's bank accounts were frozen by the AEC — as expected, the Supreme Court later seized forty-six of the seventy-six billion baht frozen by the state. All this, however, barely scratches the surface of the atrocities committed during Thaksin's regime. No charges were ever filed for the disappearances, the extra-judicial executions, and the brutal crackdown on demonstrators in the South. At the end of the day, Thaksin never paid for his real crimes. Nor will he ever.

It may be worth asking why. Why, specifically, did the generals go after Thaksin for fairly pedestrian episodes of abuse of power and weakly substantiated allegations of "policy corruption" — only to ignore potential crimes against humanity? Two reasons are typically adduced for the judiciary's inaction. Sometimes, it is argued that prosecuting these cases

---

5. "Surayud Orders Renewed Inquiry," *The Nation*, March 5, 2007.
6. Pravit Rojanaphruk, "Fugitive PM Guilty and Sentenced 2 Years in Jail," *The Nation*, October 22, 2008.

may compromise Thailand's chances of achieving "national reconciliation"[7] — as if there could be any such thing as national reconciliation without a measure of justice. In other instances, we are reminded that human rights prosecutions are complicated and messy. But though that may well apply to some of the disappearances, in cases where human remains could not be recovered, the judiciary seems determined to do nothing about the well-documented Kru Ze and Tak Bai incidents. Not to mention that the only case for which Thaksin was convicted was no slam-dunk either; the court that sentenced him to two years in prison did so on the basis of very little evidence that an actual crime had been committed.[8]

So why was nothing done to hold Thaksin accountable for the human rights abuses perpetrated on his watch? Certainly, Thaksin is responsible — quite possibly, criminally responsible — for the abuses. But it was not Thaksin who pulled the trigger on thousands of drug dealers, real and imagined. Thaksin was not present at the Kru Ze mosque. Thaksin did not physically torture Muslim youth, nor did he hide Somchai Neelaphaijit's body in the basement of his house in Thonburi. And Thaksin did not stack the demonstrators at Tak Bai into the vans that would ultimately prove to be their death chambers. All of these crimes may have been perpetrated with Thaksin's knowledge, or even at his behest; but most such monstrosities were carried out by the military and the police. So Thaksin could never be prosecuted for commissioning murders without subjecting the actual executioners to similar probes. After all, no civilized country considers the Nuremberg routine about following orders a valid reason to rape, torture, or kill. And Thailand's so-called "independent" courts, much less the junta itself, were never going to hold senior security officers accountable for their crimes.

---

[7] Sopon Ongkara, "It's Past Time to Believe there is Honour Among Thieves," *The Nation*, April 15, 2007.
8. Pravit Rojanaphruk, "No Hard Evidence against Thaksin Leaves Court in a Quandary," *The Nation*, September 17, 2008.

Consider the massacre at the Kru Ze mosque. One of the three officers whom a Pattani Provincial Court identified as responsible for the atrocities in November of 2006 is Colonel Manas Kongpan.[9] Not only was the good colonel never fired, arrested, or tried.[10] He was made the head of the Internal Security Operations Command (ISOC) in Ranong[11] — with a license to kill the wretched Rohingya refugees who landed on Thai shores, provided that the international community was looking the other way. His superior at the time the mosque was stormed, General Panlop Pinmanee — former death squad commander and erstwhile PAD supporter — was appointed by the junta as ISOC advisor after the 2006 coup.[12] Much the same goes for the carnage at Tak Bai. A decision rendered by the Songkhla Provincial Court predictably whitewashed the whole affair, concluding that "army and police officials had acted according to the law, used sound judgement and done their best given the circumstances."[13] As for the secret prisons the CIA is known to have operated in Thailand during Thaksin's administration, to this day the army adamantly denies there was ever such thing as a "black site" in Thailand.[14]

All of this points to a fairly obvious conclusion. The human rights rhetoric was useful to the military when Thaksin had to

---

9. "THAILAND: Three Army Officers Identified as Responsible for Killings," *Asian Human Rights Commission*, December 13, 2006.
10. "UPDATE (Thailand): General Responsible for Killings not Prosecuted but Reinstated," *Asian Human Rights Commission*, May 11, 2007.
11. Chalathip Thirasoonthrakul, "Thai Colonel Denies Abandoning Migrants at Sea," *Reuters*, January 21, 2009.
12. Awzar Thi, "The Ties that Bind Thailand's Burma Policy," *UPI Asia*, January 22, 2009. Incidentally, Panlop has more recently switched sides and joined Thaksin's camp.
13. "Court Clears Security Officials Over Tak Bai Deaths," *The Nation*, May 30, 2009.
14. Joby Warrick and Peter Finn, "Internal Rifts on the Road to Torment," *Washington Post*, July 18, 2009. See also: Joby Warrick and Walter Pincus, "Station Chief Made Appeals to Destroy Secret Tapes," *Washington Post*, January 16, 2008.

be overthrown, particularly as the generals sought to explain themselves in terms the international community could sympathize with. But the substance of what Thaksin had done was not particularly objectionable to them. So it was never about human rights, for which the royalist establishment has shown nothing but contempt over the past decades. Nor was it ever about corruption. Trite and increasingly half-hearted protestations to the contrary notwithstanding, the 2006 coup was about removing the threat that Thaksin posed to their own power. The ensuing prosecutions aimed exclusively to discredit Thaksin, to label him a "convicted criminal" and then a "fugitive" without seeking any actual justice or redress for his real crimes, and to establish quasi-legal grounds to seize the assets upon which, undoubtedly, any chance of a comeback would rest.

In the foreign press, Thailand is often referred to as a "constitutional monarchy" — at best a misleading characterization. Thailand is no doubt a monarchy. But whereas the country has had a host of constitutions since 1932, the institution and the authority of the monarchy exist quite independently from what the constitution *du jour* happens to provide. This should be a rather uncontroversial point — perhaps especially among Thailand's staunchest royalists. Certainly, few in Thailand would dare argue that the authority of the King could be subordinated to something so readily disposable as a Thai constitution. In a constitutional monarchy, a king ceases to be king when the constitution is rescinded — the institution, that is, exists only insofar as a constitution sanctions its existence. This is hardly the case in Thailand, where His Majesty the King reigns by something more akin to natural right than positive law. Noted royalist Pramuan Ruchanaseri said as much in a book written in 2005, where he argued — correctly, as a matter of empirical observation — that "The constitution is not above the King in any way. [...] The status of the King does not come under the constitution."[15]

---

15. Cited in Pasuk and Baker, *Thaksin*, p. 256.

The idea of constitutional monarchy is also misleading in the sense that constitutions in Thailand have historically been little more than the exterior facade of a regime whose structure and authority precede the laws chosen either to justify its rule or masquerade its existence behind the rhetoric and institutions of civilized nations. At least for the last few decades, control over government decisions has indeed been "constitutionally vested in elected officials." Real political power, however, has almost never rested with elected officials, whose autonomy is limited by the extra-constitutional domains reserved by a network of palace insiders, royal advisors, top military officers, high level bureaucrats, judges, and business elites. In academic circles, this clique is known as the "network monarchy;"[16] the expression typically used in Thailand is *amarthaya* (mandarins).

The "network monarchy" represents the most recent evolutionary stage of Thailand's ruling class. While, from the 1930s to about the late 1960s, political power was largely monopolized by the civilian and military bureaucracy,[17] the precipitous rise in royal power and prestige accomplished over the past five decades has decisively tilted the balance of power in favor of the palace, palace advisors, and the palace's network of patronage in the military, the judiciary, the civil service, and the business community. Indeed, the resurgence of the monarchy was engineered precisely by the bureaucratic polity of old, dissatisfied with the flimsy legitimacy that the constitution alone provided. When the young King Bhumibol — born in Cambridge, Massachusetts and raised in Lausanne, on the shores of Lake Geneva — unexpectedly ascended the throne in 1946 after the tragic death of his elder brother, the monarchy was in a state of disrepair. Over the previous decade, it had been stripped of many of its posses-

---

16. See Duncan McCargo, "Network Monarchy and Legitimacy Crises in Thailand," *Pacific Review* 18(2005): 499-519.
17. Fred W. Riggs, *Thailand: The Modernization of a Bureaucratic Polity* (Honolulu: University of Hawai'i Press, 1966).

sions and almost all its power, so much so that King Prajadhipok had left the country and abdicated in the years that followed the 1932 Revolution. It was military dictator Sarit Thanarat who, in the late 1950s, saw in the restoration of the monarchy's mystique an opportunity to entrench his rule.[18] Over the ensuing decades, the cause would be pursued vigorously, through schooling and aggressive legal enforcement as well as a massive, taxpayer-funded propaganda campaign that built a cult of personality quite uncharacteristic of a modern society like Thailand.

A good deal of debate exists among academics and critics of Thailand's status quo about the manner in which power is distributed within the so-called "network monarchy" — particularly between those who consider the palace to be the real locus of political power and those, like Giles Ungpakorn, who consider the monarchy's power to be quite limited, beyond the merely symbolic.[19] Ungpakorn argues not only that the palace is "weak and unprincipled," and hence easily manipulated by the military, but also that while continuing to publicly deny the monarchy's political role, the military benefits by fostering the perception that the monarchy is "all-powerful."

Certainly, His Majesty the King has never been "all-powerful" — not at the height of his reign, and certainly not now that his slow walk into the sunset is well underway. What is more, it is no doubt to the military's benefit that conservative outlets like the *Bangkok Post* continue to urge their readers to "acknowledge the omnipotence of His Majesty as the ruler of this land."[20] If, in particular, the sacrality of the monarchy has long turned the imperative to protect it into an excuse for the military's interference in Thailand's political life, on the other hand the perception that the military is acting on the

---

18. The classic statement on Sarit's motivations and strategy is offered in Thak, *Thailand: The Politics of Despotic Paternalism*.
19. For a summary, see Giles Ji Ungpakorn, "Is It Really Saying the Unsayable?," *WDPress Blog*, December 7, 2010.
20. Kong Rithdee. "Majestic Presence." *Bangkok Post*, December 3, 2010.

King's instructions gives the generals a chance to hide behind an institution that Thai law places beyond any kind of criticism. But the view of the palace as weak and easily susceptible to manipulation is also problematic. After all, to say that the King is not "all-powerful" is not to say that the monarchy is "weak" or "powerless." Having offered a slew of much less than democratic regimes the opportunity to dress up harsh dictatorial measures in a benign, paternalistic attire, the palace acquired a great deal of power by capitalizing on the military's slavish dependency on royal symbolism.

In the old days, before King Bhumibol was exalted to his current status as transcendental hero, the men who staged coups used to swing by the palace, a week or so thereafter, to "inform" the King that the generals were "returning" the powers they had seized from him. This is precisely what a delegation led by General Phin Choonhavan did in December 1951 after the "Radio Coup" of November 29.[21] Today, no military man could presume to "take over" any of the King's powers, much less would he have the impudence to "inform" him of the junta's unilateral decision to restore his prerogatives. These days, generals who want coups to be successful had better secure palace approval well in advance, and make a big enough show of groveling to His Majesty as they seek his official blessing and beg him to affix his signature on any decree the coup-makers may have drafted. In 2006, the piddling General Sonthi Boonyaratklin could never have pulled off a coup against a powerful Prime Minister without the palace's full knowledge and backing, if not at the palace's behest.

Perhaps, then, it is more accurate to say that the palace and the military coexist in a symbiosis distinguished by periodic fluctuations in the relative power exerted by each. The palace needs the military's guns to defend its influence, wealth, and prestige without taking the blame for the violence that might require. And the military needs the monarchy's symbolism

---

21. See "New Gov't Organized by Phibun," *Bangkok Post*, December 7, 1951.

to justify the barbarities it continues to perpetrate based on a cause higher than the generals' personal profit. Disagreements between the palace and the military (or factions thereof) have always existed — and have at times manifested themselves very publicly in the decades since Sarit's death. But the centrality of each institution to the other's power and survival always demanded that such differences be quickly reconciled, patched up, or swept under the rug. Invariably, the symbiotic relationship between the palace and the military has come at the expense of Thailand's democracy. As the events of the past four years have shown, the continued insistence of these institutions on exercising overriding influence over the political process remains the foremost impediment to Thailand's democratization.

To the extent that the members of the "network monarchy" — not just those who wield actual power, but also opinion makers in Thailand's media and academic community — ever acknowledge the tension between elected and unelected institutions, the continued political role played by the military and the King's mandarins is justified by the need to protect the monarchy from the threat posed by the ineptitude, corruption, and supposed republican ambitions of the country's elected representatives. To be sure, since at least the 1980s, elected representatives and ministers drawn from their ranks have enjoyed ample freedom to use their positions to get rich, help their protégés get ahead, and repay contributors for their support by plundering state coffers with impunity. What elected officials cannot do under the present circumstances is place the military under civilian control, take charge of the machinery of government, and set national policy — especially of the kind that redistributes some of the country's wealth to the provincial masses.

In fact, whether or not an elected government acts within the constitution is immaterial. It is when it begins to operate outside the confines set for it by the "network" that the country's establishment springs into action. If they can, they will use their control of the courts to overturn the results of elections through means that have the appearance of being legal. If they need to, they will send gangs of thugs into the streets to cripple the government and paralyze the country, all the while guaranteeing that the nation's laws will not apply to them. And, if they absolutely must, they will roll out the tanks and the special forces — formally taking power just long enough to write a new constitution capable of insulating them from the nuisance posed by elected officials.

Much like Chatichai before him, Thaksin was done in less by his efforts to establish an "elected dictatorship" than by his attempt to dismantle the country's "network monarchy" — in all probability, not out of disrespect or ideological distaste for the old order but out of a desire to project his government's power deep into institutions traditionally impervious to encroachments by elected officials. As he was readying his guns for entry into politics, Thaksin had been at least as keen to ingratiate himself with Thailand's unelected rulers as he had been to pummel the elected leadership of Prime Minister Chuan Leekpai and the Democrat Party. Among other things, he helped the cash-strapped Crown Property Bureau, whose holdings had been vastly diminished by the Asian Crisis, by buying out its share of ITV for $60 million — an investment he reportedly had no ambition to recover.[22] The network monarchy, at first, appeared rather satisfied with the new Prime Minister. In 2001, Prem saved Thaksin's job — pressuring the Constitutional Court to acquit him of corruption charges he had scarcely bothered denying. The Court obliged, acquitting Thaksin in a close 8-7 ruling, albeit not without some of its more disgruntled judges complaining to the press, anonymously, about the interference.[23] But it did not take long for Thaksin to turn on those he had once sought to please, or in any event, find the restrictions they placed on his government a bit too stringent for his taste.

---

22. "Royal Wealth," *Asia Sentinel*, March 1, 2007.
23. McCargo, "Network Monarchy and Legitimacy Crises," p. 513.

One constituency Thaksin never really had on his side are the civilian bureaucrats who have historically dominated Thailand's policy-making process. Even before he became Prime Minister, Thaksin was quite fond of drawing derisive, unflattering comparisons between the backward, corrupt, parasitic civil servants and the putatively modern, hard-working, productive businessmen.[24] The distrust only deepened as Thaksin rose to power and took unprecedented control of government policy. Political appointees were placed in top positions within crucial ministries to oversee both the drafting of legislation and its implementation — tasks once reserved for career bureaucrats. And the bureaucracy itself was revamped through both structural reforms and personnel decisions designed to make it more "responsive" to the elected leadership.[25] When Thaksin was done stamping out the independence of institutions such as the Election Commission, the National Counter-Corruption Commission, and the Constitutional Court, the stature and autonomy of the once-powerful civilian bureaucracy had sunk to historic lows.

The tension between Thaksin and the military is a more recent development. During his first few years in office, Thaksin had dedicated himself to restoring both the military's prestige and, to some extent, its budget. At the same time, though, Thaksin had sought to minimize the potential downsides of a resurgent military by stacking the institution with friends and cronies — elevating his own men, over the heads of officers with greater experience and seniority, to top positions they were at times manifestly unqualified to hold. The conflict with the military finally came to a head in 2005 over the yearly promotions list. This time, prominent generals took exception to Thaksin's attempt once again to impose his own people. And Privy Council President Prem Tinsulanonda, who spent decades building a network of lackeys in the military and civilian bureaucracy, was none too impressed

---

24. Pasuk and Baker, *Thaksin*, p. 172.
25. Ibid., pp. 184-188.

with Thaksin's effort to ruin his life's work. In 2005, Prem took to publicly condemning the corruption of Thaksin's regime; then, he successfully intervened in the military reshuffle and secured the crucial appointment of Sonthi Boonyaratklin to the position of Commander-in-Chief. In the run-up to the coup, Prem repeatedly put Thaksin on notice — his thinly veiled threats reminded the Prime Minister that he should not let something as trivial as an electoral mandate go to his head.

After his bone-crushing victory in the 2005 elections, however, Thaksin was much too strong to be effectively undermined, let alone removed, through any of the gentler means at the disposal of Prem and his allies. And so the military had to step in, not merely to unseat Thaksin, but lay the groundwork for his prosecution, confiscate his assets, dismantle those provisions in the 1997 constitution that protected his dominance, and put new safeguards in place against his return. When Thaksin did come back, if only by proxy, out came the right-wing thugs who softened the government's support by raising the specter of an ugly civil war. And when the people had enough of that, it was the Constitutional Court's dissolution of the People Power Party, Chat Thai, and Matchima Thipataya that finished off Somchai's administration.

The legal provisions that formed the basis of the Constitutional Court's verdict are a good illustration of the big men's *modus operandi*. Ostensibly, the legislation concerning party dissolution was included in the 2007 constitution as an instrument to tackle the country's endemic levels of electoral fraud. Under the old statute — the Organic Law on Political Parties introduced in 1998 — the Constitutional Court was only empowered to dissolve political parties found to have endangered the security of the state as well as parties deemed to have either damaged or conspired to overthrow the "democratic regime of government with the King as Head of State." Under the new laws, any party whose executive committee includes at least one member who has been disqualified for egregious violations of the law by the Election Commission of Thailand is liable to be dissolved and have its entire executive committee banned from office for a period of five years. Laws this draconian are almost unheard-of in democratic countries, where it is typically left to voters to decide which parties should survive and which should not. Even countries like India, where democracy works much better than it does in Thailand in spite of still more pervasive corruption and vote-buying, no such rule is on the books.

Given the manner in which the new statute has been enforced, it is clear that the rules on party dissolution are little more than a way for unelected institutions to restrict freedom of association in the pursuit of a distinctly undemocratic political agenda — an insurance policy of sorts against the possibility that voters might elect a government the big men dislike. It bears repeating that the Constitutional Court dissolved the People Power Party, brought about the downfall of its elected government, and disqualified its executives for five years owing to the infractions of a single man — former deputy leader and House Speaker Yongyuth Tiyaparat, found guilty of vote-buying shortly after the 2007 election.

Meanwhile, the Democrat Party and its allies have been spared a similar fate as a consequence of their own candidates' transgressions. In October 2008, Democrat executive Vithoon Nambutr was absolved by the ECT in connection with an episode of alleged vote-buying that involved the distribution of free movie tickets in Ubon Ratchatani. For that same infraction, the ECT imposed sanctions on two Democrat MPs who were not members of the executive committee.[26] More troubling still, Deputy Interior Minister Boonjong Wongtrairat (of the Bhum Jai Thai party), who admitted to handing out, at his own home, $3000 in public funds to two hundred villagers in Nakorn Ratchasima — enclosing business cards — was found by the ECT to have violated no law. One can-

---

26. Mongkol Bangprapa and Manop Thip-Osod, "Democrats Safe from Dissolution," *Bangkok Post*, October 28, 2008.

TYRANNY OF THE BIG MEN   83

not be accused of buying votes if no election campaign is officially in progress.[27] And Peua Paendin, a party bribed into splitting with Thaksin's camp after the PPP was dissolved, was let off on the grounds that Noppadol Polsue, an executive committee member found guilty of vote-buying in the run-up to the 2007 election, was not a member of the party's executive at the time he committed the offenses.[28] Even so, the ECT threatened PPP successor Peua Thai with dissolution, should the party have moved forward with a proposal that is not even explicitly banned by the constitution — appointing Thaksin Shinawatra to an advisory position — as the appointment may have been found to "adversely affect the country's stability."[29]

Meanwhile, nobody at the ECT so much as batted an eye when it was reported, in the days since the PAD was ordered by its patrons to vacate Suvarnabhumi airport, that banned politician Newin Chidchob was openly negotiating with Democrat Party leader Abhisit Vejjajiva the terms (and price) of his parliamentary faction's support of the new government. A former Thaksin loyalist and arguably Thailand's foremost vote-buyer,[30] Newin Chidchob is a Buriram-based politician whose clout and aspirations survived, intact, the five-year ban from politics imposed on Thai Rak Thai executives in the aftermath of the 2006 coup. After days of feverish negotiations with the Democrats, it was announced in early December 2008 that Newin had engineered the defection of his faction of thirty-some MPs — the aptly named "Friends of Newin," now reconstituted in Bhum Jai Thai — paving the way for Abhisit's assumption of the prime ministerial post.

---

27. Mongkol Bangprapa, "EC Absolves Boonjong of Power Abuse," *Bangkok Post*, July 5, 2009.
28. "Puea Pandin Saved from Dissolution," *Bangkok Post*, July 30, 2009.
29. "EC Warns Pheu Thai Over Appointing Thaksin," *The Nation*, January 18, 2009.
30. Chang Noi, "When the Beauty of Democracy is Not So Beautiful," *The Nation*, December 22, 2008.

The vote held in the House of Representatives, just days after the news of the backroom deal broke, promised to be a nail-biter. Peua Thai, a party that had long been set up to inherit the People Power Party's members and contributors in the event that its widely anticipated dissolution was indeed to be handed down, put forth Police General Pracha Promnok. Almost everyone else seemed to have pledged their support to Abhisit — someone voters had rejected when they were given the chance to choose for themselves. When the votes were counted, Abhisit defeated Pracha 235-198. Thaksin lost a key battle. Anupong demonstrated that the army, though reluctant to intervene directly, could still neuter democratic institutions and impose its own men. Most importantly, Newin showed other faction leaders that they could now return to exerting the independence and clout they had lost under the old boss. Thanks to the usual suspects' interference in the democratic process, Newin's move promised to mark the end of a brief era in Thai politics where parties had seemed to matter more than factions.

By-elections held less than a month later dealt a further blow to the integrity of Thaksin's coalition. Considering Newin's betrayal, retaining ten of the People Power Party's thirteen seats up for a re-vote was not a terrible result. Nor could the performance of the competition be considered much of a setback. Chat Thai Pattana — the reconstituted Chat Thai, itself cajoled into supporting Abhisit — basically held steady. The Democrat Party performed well in central Thailand as well as the North, netting seven additional seats. But the Democrats were no more a national party than they had been in 2007. And their victory in constituencies where Democrat candidates had placed respectably in the past may simply have reflected a modicum of good will towards Abhisit in the wake of his rise to Prime Minister — tenuous gains that threatened quickly to evaporate as his government set about tackling difficult problems. Peua Thai was indeed in trouble, but for reasons more profound than the number of seats it had won or lost.

Back in the day when the old boss was still in power, Thai Rak Thai had been built into a force far greater than the sum of its personalities. The best known part of the story is that the 2001 elections were a watershed event, marking a sharp break with Thailand's recent past that was soon to trigger a decisive re-organization of the country's party system. In 2001, Thai Rak Thai took 248 seats, just two shy of an absolute majority in the House of Representatives. Over the ensuing four years, Thaksin embarked on a successful effort to make Thai Rak Thai the dominant force in Thai politics — to destroy any chance of government alternation by co-opting the leaders, factions, and politicians of all major parties except the Democrats. Fresh rounds of elections in 2005 were a testament to the party's newfound supremacy. Thai Rak Thai won three-quarters of the lower house seats. The Democrats were forced to retreat deeper into their strongholds on the Malay peninsula. Of the other parties remained but the carcasses, desolately strewn outside of the halls of parliament.

In the space of less than a decade, Thailand's political scene had undergone a remarkable transformation. What were once little more than legal shells for a bewildering number of internally fluid parliamentary factions dominated by local notables had seemingly crystallized around two alternatives — one of which, by 2005, seemed increasingly implausible as a governing party. In addition, whereas Thai Rak Thai's growth, as measured in seat shares, attests to a reduction in the number of parties, these numbers fail to tell an equally important side of the story. Thai Rak Thai, that is, was much more of a "real" party than any of its predecessors. Its organizational structure was highly centralized; its parliamentary wing sternly enforced party discipline through tough hardball tactics. Local politicians remained important for mobilizing votes in the provinces, but they were no longer the locus of the party's financial and organizational resources. And while as many as fifteen factions operated within TRT, their importance, power, and independence were quashed under Thaksin's leadership.[31]

Once he was sworn in as Prime Minister, Thaksin had taken a novel approach to consolidating his party. His predecessors Chuan, Barnharn, and Chavalit had sought to build "minimum winning coalitions" that would maximize the share of benefits and cabinet positions available for apportionment to their support-cast of parties and factions. Minimum winning coalitions, however, were unstable because the parties and factions included in the majority had a clear incentive to withdraw their support and join the parties currently in the opposition whenever they sensed an opportunity to get a better deal by forming a different government. For various reasons, Chuan, Barnharn, and Chavalit had been done in by their governments' inter- and intra-party divisions.

Thaksin went at it a completely different way. Rather than leave his coalition vulnerable to the defection of small parties and factions, he endeavored to put together a super-majority that could withstand any such desertion. Parties like New Aspiration and Seritham dissolved themselves into Thai Rak Thai, while Thaksin also secured the participation in the governing alliance of all other parties except the Democrats. In the process, Thaksin had greatly reduced the power of factions within his own government. Now endowed with a super-majority, any party or faction that pulled its support would accomplish nothing but lose whatever positions it currently controlled. Thaksin had effectively killed the cycle of instability in the House by forming what the political science literature calls a "predominant party."

The question remains, however, why the parties and factions that saw their influence and independence shrink with every merger and the addition of every new coalition member did not desert Thaksin and put together a government that

---

31. Paul Chambers,"Evolving Toward What? Parties, Factions, and Coalition Behavior in Thailand Today," *Journal of East Asian Studies* 5(2005): 495-520, p. 514.

would guarantee them a larger share of the pie. In this regard, it certainly helped that Thaksin paid his MPs rather handsomely for their support — somewhere in the neighborhood of $5,000 per month plus a bonus of at least $20,000 awarded during various festivities and millions of baht for their campaigns.[32] Even more significant is the assistance that Thaksin was offered by provisions in the 1997 constitution. First, given that cabinet ministers had to resign their legislative seats, exiting the coalition would now amount to leaving elected office altogether. Any such defection was therefore costly. Second, the Prime Minister could now call elections at forty-five days' notice, but the new rules required each candidate to have been a member of a party for at least ninety days prior to the elections. Factions that would desert the government, precipitating the dissolution of the House, would be left out in the cold for an entire legislative cycle.

As Thaksin added more components to his party and his coalition, the stability of his government increased and the possibility of having the tables turned on him vastly diminished. In turn, as the ability of the opposition to lure coalition members out of the government was neutralized, the pressure intensified for the remaining opposition parties to join the government themselves. More and more parties jumped on Thaksin's bandwagon, even at the cost of sacrificing much of the independence they once enjoyed.

Shrewdly enough, Thaksin capitalized on the stranglehold he had over factions within Thai Rak Thai and its main allies through the swift implementation of his trademark policies. And while these policies proved highly controversial because of the way the government paid for them as well as their dubious effectiveness, they were immensely popular with provincial voters and the urban poor. The popularity of these programs, in turn, allowed Thai Rak Thai to "take credit for improvements in the lives of villagers, at the expense of the provincial and local notables who had previously charac-

---

32. Pasuk and Baker, *Thaksin*, p. 192.

terized such resource allocation as personal rather than party patronage."[33] In so doing, Thaksin further solidified his electoral support and enhanced the power of Thai Rak Thai's central administration over provincial politicians. Whereas parties had once depended on notables to win provincial races, it was now local politicians who could hardly envision being re-elected without Thai Rak Thai's endorsement. By 2005, Thaksin had cannibalized virtually every component of his alliance.

In the wake of Abhisit's rise to Prime Minister, the streamlining that Thailand's fractious party system had undergone over the previous decade appeared to be coming undone. If Thai Rak Thai was once able to soundly defeat local notabilities who failed to sign on, to the point where even generally non-partisan local elections had begun to witness stiff competition for the use of the party's label, the January 2009 by-elections demonstrated that Peua Thai had lost its ascendancy. Puea Thai did well in Isan, but it actually lost, badly, old Thai Rak Thai bastions in Buriram and Ubon Ratchathani. Aside from the strong showing of the Democrats, who benefited from their enhanced national role, many voters in the Northeast and central Thailand simply went with the local politicians sponsored by Barnharn and Newin's well-oiled patronage machines. Peua Thai now seemed powerless against its defectors — Newin's faction, Peua Paendin, and Chat Thai Pattana having paid no price for their betrayal. And it was itself much more dependent on its own factions and local notables to win seats in supposed strongholds. Even the fact that the ten seats won by the opposition to Abhisit Vejjajiva were now shared between Peua Thai and Pracharaj did not bode well for the cohesion of the coalition Thaksin built — what was left of it, anyway. The long knives were out and scintillating brightly in an otherwise dark night for Thailand's democracy.

It goes without saying that the improbable return to prom-

---

33. Ockey, *Making Democracy*, p. 50.

inence of parliamentary factions owed much to the concerted efforts of the palace, the Privy Council, the military, and the PAD. The 2006 coup had done little either to reduce Thaksin's popularity or to loosen his authority over former Thai Rak Thai politicians. During his prolonged absence from the country, Thaksin's coalition remained remarkably robust — so much so that when the military returned to the barracks the People Power Party won the 2007 elections quite handily. Newin's defection evidenced that Thaksin's once-unshakable grip was more tenuous than it had been at any point since 2001. His enemies had adapted. Instead of overthrowing the government, they succeeded in thoroughly undermining the People Power Party's administration. By denying the administration's capacity to provide the kind of social order that is every government's first responsibility, they highlighted for many people in Thailand the futility, if not the danger, of sticking with anti-establishment parties at a time when the country faced grave challenges on many fronts. In the process, they made defections from the newly formed Peua Thai less costly to former Thai Rak Thai politicians with ambitions of their own.

The prospective return to the status quo ante, where factions matter more than parties and parties come and go with each new round of elections, is not all bad news. Lest we forget, it was Thaksin's ability to reverse the long-standing fragmentation of Thailand's party system that also allowed him to pursue appallingly anti-democratic policies. On balance, however, it would be hard not to describe this development as anything but a serious step back for democracy — not to mention a stunning success for institutions like the palace and the military, whose leaders have actively worked against each and every one of Thailand's ill-fated, democratically elected governments.

Of course, if it would now take the defection of a mere twenty men to turn the tables on Abhisit's very own "nominee government," their machinations could be said to have accomplished little — having merely produced another gridlocked coalition running the risk of falling apart on every decision it would be forced to make. But while the presence of fractious, factionalized parties is what keeps Thai politics stuck in conditions of legislative paralysis, rampant corruption, and cabinet instability, this situation does offer yet more evidence that Thailand needs the palace and the military to save it from the loathsome, back-stabbing politicians its misguided, child-like population continues to elect. And if the absence of a democratic counterweight allows unelected, anti-democratic institutions to call the shots on every matter of significance — just as they have for the past several decades — the chronic ineffectiveness of democratically elected governments further strengthens the military and the palace in their self-appointed role as the guarantors of reason, stability, and order.

There are at least two profound ironies in all this. The first is that institutions supposedly charged with serving and protecting the country basically held a gun to the head of the Thai people, telling them that so long as they did not vote the establishment wanted the PAD could hold the entire nation hostage with impunity. Predictably, the people responded by choosing the path of least resistance, meekly acquiescing to the big men's implicit, but transparent enough commands. The other irony is that while palace, the military, and the PAD grounded their opposition to Thaksin in their abhorrence of patronage, corruption, and vote-buying, the renewed salience of factions and local notables at the expense of "real" political parties promised to make patronage, corruption, and vote-buying even more central to future election campaigns. Indeed, it is now apparent that Thaksin's real crime was not vote-buying — though he no doubt engaged in a great deal of it. The real crime was rather that Thaksin no longer really needed to buy votes to win elections.

The self-righteous urban elites, meanwhile, raised no objection when Newin's "Friends" were bought, in bulk, on behalf of Abhisit's government. Indeed, Prem and Anupong at least facilitated, if not directly orchestrated, the entire transaction. Anupong essentially placed the weight of his tanks, as *The Nation* bragged in an article naming him person of the year, behind his attempt to get just enough majority MPs to jump the fence[34] — by some coalition politicians' own admission, going as far as organizing a meeting at his own home on December 6 to "advise" those who still wavered. Aside from the explicit coup threats, what sealed the deal was probably that Anupong had made it clear he was "conveying a message from a man who could not be refuted."[35]

It did not hurt that the defectors were promised the usual lucrative cabinet positions. Or that the powerful business allies of every party involved in the negotiations chipped in with some cold, hard cash. King Power International Group, whose airport concessions were under threat, had a key interest in Newin's participation in the new government — the increasingly disillusioned Sondhi Limthongkul has himself accused its executives of having made large payments to sweeten the deal.[36] And in November, before any talk of an Abhisit-led executive was widely publicized, companies associated with key establishment figures had donated 120 million baht to the Democrat Party, which had only raised a combined thirty million over the previous ten months.[37] Among the benefactors is True Corporation, a subsidiary of mega business conglomerate Charoen Pokphand Group. CP Group executive Virachai Viramethakul, whom Democrat leader Suthep Thaugsuban praised for being "instrumental in gathering support from defecting MPs for the Democrats' bid

---

34. "Masters of the Game," *The Nation*, December 29, 2008.
35. "Democrat Govt a Shotgun Wedding?," *The Nation*, December 10, 2009.
36. "Suthep, Sondhi War of Words Widens," *Bangkok Post*, March 11, 2009.
37. Kornchanok Raksaseri, "Democrats see Bt120m Windfall," *Bangkok Post*, December 22, 2008.

to form the new government,"[38] was given a cabinet position. It was later reported that Virachai had paid eighty million baht for his post, in an undeclared donation that the Democrat Party would have certainly put to good use.[39]

This sordid affair speaks to more than simple hypocrisy on the part of palace and the military, which obviously abhor corruption only when it benefits people they do not like. It speaks rather to their broader agenda and strategy. It is quite apparent, in particular, that the military and the palace have no interest in ruling the country directly — in such a way that they can be held accountable for what they do in office (at least by public opinion if not through elections). As it turns out, Thak Chaloemtiarana was right to predict that the increased complexity of Thai society would render the prospect of direct, long-term military rule more implausible than five or even three decades ago.[40]

The emptiness of Anupong's repeated coup threats was a clear indication that the establishment wants no repeat of the 2006 fiasco, which it undertook reluctantly in the first place. The generals and the King's mandarins, however, have not let go of the idea that they should call the shots behind the scenes. And, on this count, the biggest challenge to their continued dominance is not Thaksin or even Thai Rak Thai, but rather the emergence of *any* strong national political party that takes its electoral mandate seriously. So long as Thai politics remains factionalized, corrupt, and patronage-based, the ability of the palace and the military to run the show remains intact. At the same time, should anyone call them out on it, they can always point to the ineptitude and corruption of elected politicians as evidence that powerful unelected institutions are actually needed to protect Thailand from the

---

38. Piyanart Srivalo, "Grumbling in the Ranks," *Bangkok Post*, December 19, 2008.
39. "Pheu Thai to Act against Abhisit," *The Nation*, December 22, 2008.
40. Thak, *Thailand: The Politics of Despotic Paternalism*, p. xv.

inanity of its own citizens.

Of course, Thailand's problem is not that it has had too much democracy, as His Majesty the King argued in the wake of the 1976 massacre, but rather that what little democracy it has experienced since 1932 has been systematically undermined and subverted whenever it produced results its unelected masters did not like. Never having been given the chance to develop into a functioning system of government, democracy has cyclically produced the kind of inept, fragmented administrations that made the rise of a brash, decisive, populist leader like Thaksin Shinawatra possible in the first place.

It is perhaps natural, in this sense, that Thailand's real power holders and their propagandists in the local press would want to cloak their "dictatorship of the big men" in the benign, legitimizing language of democratic development. But whatever the constitution might say, the real story of the last seventy-five years is not the "development" of democracy. It is rather the methodical sabotage of any meaningful democratic development, the routine hijacking of democratic institutions, and the continued suffocation of Thailand's democratic aspirations orchestrated by an unelected ruling class in an attempt to entrench its power — all the while, rendering itself increasingly unaccountable to the Thai masses and the international community. Now that their military coups, their intimidation, and their preposterous judicial decisions based on blinding double standards seemed to have finally broken Thaksin's coalition, these same old men could safely return to their same old scam — making democracy so useless that the Thai people could not possibly ask for more of it.

There was a vast amount of criminality in London, a whole world-within-a-world of thieves, bandits, prostitutes, drug-peddlers, and racketeers of every description; but since it all happened among the proles themselves, it was of no importance. In all questions of morals they were allowed to follow their ancestral code. The sexual Puritanism of the Party was not imposed upon them. Promiscuity went unpunished, divorce was permitted. For that matter, even religious worship would have been permitted if the proles had shown any sign of needing or wanting it. They were beneath suspicion. As the Party slogan put it: "Proles and animals are free."

—GEORGE ORWELL
Nineteen Eighty-Four

FOUR

THAILAND FOR SALE

> This good and modern road is the sign of economic development and the building of a new 'face' for the country, which should make us all very proud.
>
> —SARIT THANARAT[1]

Soi 4, just off Sukhumvit Road, has all the gloss and silky smoothness of a chunk of pulsating, raw flesh. The uniquely Thai blend of fermenting piss, rotting compost, exhaust fumes, and burnt-out cooking oils is only rendered more asphyxiating by the cheap incense smoldering by the ubiquitous makeshift shrine. Steam rises from the roadside food-stalls that cramp the narrow, potholed sidewalk; it is with difficulty that it finally dissipates into the thick, damp air. A bewildering lineup of dead animals on a stick lie on display on pushcarts, alongside tropical fruit whose freshness has long evaporated on the foggy plexiglass shielding it from the flies and the dust. Whole roasted chickens sit on bare tables next to fake eyelashes and make-up, flanked by rows of size-zero tank-tops and lingerie. Typically most transfixing to newcomers and repeat offenders alike, however, is the repugnant assortment of deep-fried crickets, roaches, locusts, and other

---

1. Remarks at the opening ceremony for Sukhumvit Rd. Cited in Thak, *Thailand: The Politics of Despotic Paternalism*, p. 153.

bugs sold here by the bagful. They are a favorite with the go-go dancer, who can at times be spotted crunching lazily on the six-legged critters — occasionally plucking the limb of a grasshopper impudently lodged between her front teeth.

It is not long after dusk, but the place is swarming. A rag-tag army of hustlers and beggars is out in full force. Middle-aged females sprawled out on the wet pavement pull at every pant leg within their limited reach, imploring passers-by to look at the filthy, emaciated children sleeping in their arms. Men with mutilated limbs shove their stumps into startled white faces for dramatic effect. A blind, deranged man in tattered clothes stumbles through the crowd, holding a cup half-filled with coins that jangle loudly as he violently bumps shoulders with pedestrians briskly walking past him. Touts selling Viagra, teddy bears, and cheap knock-offs of brand-name wrist watches and sunglasses hassle every foreigner they come across, often placing the items in their prospective customer's hands — as if to make the ill-advised purchase a *fait accompli*. Fat American women take turns having their pictures taken atop a small elephant. Nearby, a six-foot tall ladyboy poses with a Middle-Eastern tourist shrouded in a black burqa. On the other side of the street, a stray dog looks on, crippled and scarred, as if unsure of his next move, perplexed by the feeding frenzy unfolding before his very eyes. Rummaging through trash is a tough business in this part of town.

"Haah-rrooow, weeeear-come, where you go sexy man?" The endlessly repeated mantra echoes all around, mixing in a thunderous cacophony with the thumping sounds of techno, disco, and hip-hop, the languid falsetto flamed out by a Thai pop star, and the dire opening notes of Gimme Shelter blasted from the crackling loudspeakers of the Morning and Night Bar.

They are everywhere. Free-lancers stand shoulder-to-shoulder on sidewalks and alleyways. Others prepare for another long night of somewhat less than backbreaking work.

They pack what little seating is available by the foodstalls and clutter the brightly lit convenience stores in a last-minute search for chewing gums, cigarettes, condoms, vaginal lubricant, lottery tickets, and travel-sized toiletries — the requisite tools of the trade. Still others lovingly pay homage to mysterious celestial beings, genuflecting with evident devotion before a spirit house adorned with garlands, plastic action heroes, butter cookies, and freshly opened bottles of bubblegum-flavored Fanta surrounded by swarms of flies. It is only upon completing the elaborate preparatory ritual that they finally report for duty, making their way into the go-go bars or alternatively joining their colleagues atop worn-out stools lining the wooden barroom verandas.

Nana Entertainment Plaza — in much of the country, the word "entertainment" serves as a euphemism for anything designed to end in ejaculation — is a disheveled three-story bazaar of cascading go-go bars, glaring red neons, and mildewy guestrooms rented out by the romp. Acts of unutterable depravity are committed or tentatively agreed upon here. Men who seeped through the bowels of every first world society drip all the way down here to feast on a banquet of oriental game. Barely post-pubescent, bronze-skinned metrosexuals join limp septuagenarians carrying lifetime supplies of indispensable hard-on pills. Veteran sex fiends wear as decorations from previous, valiant campaigns t-shirts acquired in places as far flung as Cambodia, the Philippines, Brazil, Costa Rica, and the Dominican Republic. Most belong to the thick sludge of balding middle-aged men, tourist and expatriate alike, flaunting their trademark deformity — guts swollen from a lifetime of the old lady's home-cooking and an eternity spent lounging in the slothful comfort of a livingroom couch.

Much like their patrons, the working girls come in all shapes and sizes. Most have the brown or burnt orange complexion of the Lao and Khmer peoples of Isan, the vast wasteland of depressed northeastern provinces surviving on reliably meager rice crops, occasional handouts distributed by local officeholders, and a steady flow of remittances drenched in the bodily fluids of all manners of Western creeps. They are not all young, nor are they all pretty. Nor, for that matter, are they all women. With a few, blinding exceptions easily explained by the bulge in the man's back pocket, the girls are rather well-matched with their employers *du jour*. Those whose looks afford them the luxury pride themselves on picking their dates discerningly, with a keen eye to physical appearance, dress, charm, and any information about net worth one might glean from a man's consumption, mannerisms, and eagerness to part company with money for no reason whatsoever.

The pocket-sized *Lonely Planet* guidebook that accompanies scores of tourists on their first, wide-eyed trip down here proclaims, in an exercise of misplaced self-flattery, that "beautiful [Thai] women will throw themselves at you, all for a modest sum (money or status)." That men of wealth, status, and taste would have privileged access to beautiful women hardly distinguishes Thailand from any other country on earth. The operative word is "modest"— what counts as money and status here gets one a stack of food stamps and a welfare check back home. For many Westerners, however, Bangkok's legendary magnetism does not lie in its heavily discounted market rates. It is rather that the services rendered in this town involve a measure of passion and lust that prostitutes elsewhere typically do not offer.

For the local bargirl, after all, a long term relationship with a *farang* is prospectively the most secure of early retirement funds. Most are well aware that the clock is ticking inexorably on their capacity to earn incomes equivalent to those paid to mid-level corporate management in Thailand's private sector — and several times the salary of most government workers. To make matters worse, their lifestyle mercilessly accelerates the aging process, rendering them thoroughly washed up by age thirty. And when the music stops, in a few short years, a life less glamorous still awaits those left without a foreign husband. Not many among them look forward to working night shifts in a factory, giving $5 handjobs in a seedy massage parlor, or sweating blood in the fields upcountry.

So rather than settle for a single-night shakedown of the worthless pigs, the girls often take a more calculating, long-term approach to dealing with Westerners. After all, the typical working girl is smart enough to run circles around the slow-breathing prole or petty bourgeois that is your average sex tourist or expatriate. They may not have the faintest idea of what they are getting into — most foreigners here posing a varying measure of danger to themselves and others — but many jump at the chance of taking the devil they do not know. Indeed, the instant cuddling may be somewhat unauthentic, the words they whisper a bit sappy, and the loud, writhing orgasms a tad contrived, but the attempt to get them to care is sincere enough. You may call it "the fierce urgency of now." And that makes for a damn good time, one would guess, for those so fortunate as to be singled out as a potential one-way ticket out of the cesspool or, at the very minimum, a temporary shelter from its sickening stench.

While some might soon internalize the detachment required to keep philandering fun, costless, and risk-free, many men never quite get the chance. The biggest losers revel in the single-minded attention lavished on them by their cheap conquests. At last, their *joie de vivre* has staged an improbable comeback, rekindled by the renewed certainty in a measure of cosmic justice that comes in the flesh and blood of a twenty-something Thai hooker — a true Siamese cat of a girl eager to suck cocks no matter how puny, wrinkled, or flaccid. A week in Bangkok makes humble men proud. Even for the less desperate, though, spending a few days with a Thai working girl is often all it takes to become thoroughly confused about her motives, to begin to wonder whether romantic considerations could have indeed replaced the pecuniary. Of course, this dichotomy of motivations is often fallacious, for one only precludes the other in the facile mental schema with which the Western obtuse makes sense of the world around him.

The anthropologist Erik Cohen had it about right when he noted that there is "often no crisp separation in Thai society between emotional and mercenary sexual relationships."[2] If anything, it is more complicated than that. Specifically, while it is the girls themselves who frequently push relationships held together by regular side payments to quickly develop some emotional content — animated bouts of jealousy, profanity-laced tirades, crying fits, physical abuse, and even the stray assault with a deadly weapon are far from uncommon after just a handful of encounters — at the same time the girls go to some lengths to compartmentalize the demands of their careers from other aspects of their lives. And while they are aware of the stigma with which their profession brands them, they are quite keen to protest their modesty upon being characterized as loose or promiscuous.

Quite aside from what the girls more or less purposively do to turn a quick in-and-out into a sultrier, more protracted affair, the stories they tell are frequently poignant enough to drive a dagger into the soft spots of even the most irreparably jaded, cynical, or sociopathic. A common thread runs through the dismal narratives. In the background is a large or broken family. The surviving parents are always poor, sometimes abusive, and occasionally in the throes of an addiction to alcohol, gambling, or methamphetamine. As soon as she is old enough to make it on her own, if still much too young to do anything useful with her life, the girl drops out of school and moves to the big city.

The poor bitch, no education, marketable skills, or social graces to boot, comes to Bangkok to face quite the conundrum. One option is to work twelve hours a day in a convenience store, serve tables at a restaurant, or scrub the latrines of a hotel, shopping center, or private home. That only gets

---

2. Erik Cohen, "Thai Girls and Farang Men: The Edge of Ambiguity," *Annals of Tourism Research: A Social Sciences Journal* 9(1982): 403-428, 406.

her about six thousand baht (no more than $200) per month. And after paying rent for a shared hole-in-the-wall, not much is left for herself or her family.

The alternative is to sleep until mid-afternoon, lounge around for a while, take a leisurely promenade shopping for faux name-brand clothes and accessories, and finally make it to the bar at a late hour of her choice. At work, have a drink or two, suit up in boots and bikini, take twenty-minute turns "dancing" — more like wobbling listlessly around the pole with all the conviction and energy evocative of Shakira on Xanax — and find some foreigner to screw at the fixed rates that apply to short-time and long-time romps. Between the regular salary paid by the bar, the commissions on "barfines" and "lady drinks," and a hundred percent of the fees paid by the customer directly to the girl, a fraction of the effort, to say nothing of the abuse and humiliation, generates an income at least five times as large as that guaranteed by 7-Eleven. If the girl is pretty, charming, and has a strong enough stomach to service multiple strangers a day, her monthly income might exceed $3,000 — more than what a decent chunk of her own customers make. More empowering still, the status of a young girl otherwise as authoritative as the water buffalo parked underneath the stilted family home in the provinces soars as she becomes the family's chief breadwinner.

Beyond this skeletal plot, variations on both theme and cast of characters are legion. Many of the girls have one or more children living with their grandparents in Isan. Their eyes well up when they are pushed to admit that the kids no longer recognize their mother — much less pay attention to anything she has to say — when they go back for a rare visit once or twice a year. Mom or dad might have initiated the girl to the time-honored trade by selling her virginity to an acquaintance of their choice. Ever present is also a younger sibling whose studies are subsidized by the big sister turning tricks in the big town. But it is the dangerous Thai ex-boyfriend who is invariably the most interesting character. He might enter the storyline as a thug, a drug dealer, or a deadbeat dad. Or he might just be the girl's first love, the man who broke her heart when he walked out with someone else, got thrown in jail, or better yet, perished in a barroom brawl, a drug overdose, or an all-out shootout with the police.

It is upon learning of such deplorable lives that the foreigner might begin to fathom the once imponderable eventuality of shacking up with a whore, making it his mission to rescue the girl from a life of poverty and ignorance. Many meet this pathetic fate here. So it is no doubt with a large measure of astonishment that newcomers first notice just how many have ceased to wear the giddy, inebriated expression one would imagine etched onto every man's face in such a generously discounted themepark for the self-indulgent. Much to the bemusement and sometimes the chagrin of the locals, thousands of Western men stroll Bangkok's bustling streets and shopping malls, watching over rented girlfriends and hired wives with the dreamy, loving eyes of someone who, against all logic, self-respect, and sound advice, at some point began to care.

The *farang* is not much loved here — at least not at the highest rungs of Thailand's social ladder. The word itself — a derivative of Frank, as in the barbaric tribe that swept through northern France after the demise of the Roman Empire — is used, somewhat disparagingly, to describe the amorphous, undifferentiated mob of barbarous white men and the relentlessly mocked contingent of corpulent, unkept white women. Beyond the miscellany of geo-political grievances that the editorial pages of Thailand's English-language newspapers persistently, if rather inelegantly, articulate, the resentment is often well-deserved. After all, the white man's immorality and boorishness is on permanent display in this city — at every hour of the day and night.

Even as far back as the sixteenth century, Dutch traders sojourning in the old Siamese capital Ayutthaya had a penchant for taking local concubines — fathering multiple children to be readily abandoned upon one's return to Europe. So many Dutchmen left fatherless children in Ayutthaya, it seems, that an orphanage of sorts appears to have been in operation for the sole purpose of attending to the half-bred.[3] By the nineteenth century, when the Kingdom of Siam witnessed a substantial influx of Western merchants, artists, engineers, and bureaucrats, close to every last one of them had one or more Thai mistresses, some apparently going as far as maintaining harems.[4] And it is well know that at least since the halcyon days of the Vietnam War — when a corrupt military government drooling for foreign aid and investment rented out to American servicemen its least valuable human resources — Westerners in Thailand have been strictly on their worst behavior.

Of course, the fact that foreigners are the most conspicuous and shameless consumers of homegrown young flesh does not mean they are either the most numerous or the most irredeemably depraved partakers in this bountiful sector of Thailand's vast semi-submerged economy. One would never tell by simply walking around Bangkok, but those in the know remind us that ninety-five percent of the country's notorious sex industry caters strictly to Thai men.[5] Thai men, however, do not particularly like to be seen hiring hookers. Those at the very high end of the scale patronize "entertainment" and "massage" venues that line major thoroughfares like Rachadapisek and Phetchaburi Road — places ostentatiously known as Caesar's, Emmanuelle, Cleopatra, and Poseidon. The buildings are imposing and grandiose, with ample parking out back. Inside, men choose from dozens of girls sitting

---

3. Chris Baker et al., *Van Vliet's Siam* (Chiang Mai: Silkworm Books, 2005).
4. Tamara Loos, *Subject Siam: Family, Law, and Colonial Modernity in Thailand* (Chiang Mai: Silkworm Books, 2006), p. 104.
5. Jeremy Seabrook, *Travels in the Skin Trade: Tourism and the Sex Industry* (London: Pluto Press, 1996), p. 79; see also Leslie Ann Jeffrey, *Sex and Borders: Gender, National Identity, and Prostitution Policy in Thailand* (Chiang Mai: Silkworm Books, 2002), p. 40.

in "fishbowls" separated from the clientele by thick, sometimes one-way glass. Also on offer, though hidden from view, are models said to have posed in the Thai editions of famous magazines. Once the charges are settled — all major credit cards accepted — the two-hour dalliance takes place in lavish rooms endowed with jacuzzis, king-sized beds, and plentiful mirrors.

These places of merriment operate quite openly, thanks to the relaxation in the anti-prostitution laws that occurred in the context of an aggressive promotion of tourism in the 1960s — from all-out prohibition to the legalization of entertainment venues where women offer unspecified "special services." The ambiguity of the law and the arbitrariness proper to any kind of law enforcement in Thailand, however, still leaves the possibility that these places of widely known disrepute may be subject to official harassment. So it does not hurt to cultivate a clientele of powerful businessmen and politicians. Or to enter politics directly. Lek Nana himself, once the owner of the land upon which Nana Plaza stands, was one of the founders and financiers of the ruling Democrat Party. When he died in April 2010, his casket was buried in soil donated by His Majesty the King, presumably in recognition of his service to the country.[6] And current Commerce Minister Pornthiva Nakasai, the highest-ranking woman in Abhisit Vejjajiva's government, was offered a cabinet post on the basis of her experience as the owner and long-time manager of Poseidon, arguably Bangkok's most renowned brothel.

For good measure, cash by the truckload is doled out to policemen at every link of the chain of command. Chuwit Kamolvisit, once one of the city's most powerful pimps and more recently twice a candidate for governor, confirmed back in 2004 what everyone already knew. That he paid twelve million baht (some $400,000) per month to police and offered five million baht in free services to keep just a handful of plac-

---

6. "King Gives Soil for Democrat Founder's Burial," *The Nation*, April 2, 2010.

es running — as he claimed in an interview with the *Guardian* newspaper[7] — is astounding not so much for the corruption it reveals, but rather because it hints at just how immense his profits would have been.

Though priced at a relatively modest $80-$200, these establishments are well beyond the reach of most Thai men. For the petty bourgeois, the best available alternative is to enlist the services of the streetwalkers who congregate around Suan Lum Night Bazaar, the strip of discos and nightclubs around Rama IX Road, and other areas spared the influx of foreigners, where one might get serviced for as little as $10-20. Many of the girls working this beat are said to be college students dabbling in the trade for some extra *argent de poche*. Nearby, a wealth of short-time motels are equipped with curtains that can be drawn around each parked car so as to conceal make, model, and license plate from prying eyes. For those who still cannot afford these, the country is littered with dirt-cheap "tea houses," "massage parlors," and "karaokes" fronting for brothels where the company of frequently underage, immigrant girls kept in conditions of semi-bondage can be enjoyed for a nominal fee.

It may be worth noting that monogamy, at least as a legal construct, is a recent import to Thailand. Though de facto restricted to noblemen and, more recently, to commoners who had risen to top positions in the bureaucracy, among such groups polygyny was practiced well into the twentieth century. King Chulalongkorn, aptly regarded as Thailand's greatest monarch, fathered seventy-seven children from as many as 150 "minor" wives bestowed upon him by families desperately seeking royal favor. When it was proscribed in 1935, after decades of debate that gradually spilled from the small circle of the King's closest advisers into the public arena, the practice had long ceased to play its historical function. By the turn of the century, the replacement of a system of feudal vassalage

---

7. Cathy Scott-Clark and Adrian Levy, "The Brothel King's Revenge," *The Guardian*, February 21, 2004.

with an absolute monarchy commanding a bureaucratic and military apparatus extending deep into the provinces had rendered the system largely superfluous.

The sole purpose that polygyny now served, it seems, was to quench the nobleman's taste for variety and parade his virility for the whole world to see. The government went so far as to craft rambling defenses of polygamy as a symbol of religious and national identity — the best they could do on this count was to note that the practice is nowhere explicitly prohibited in Buddhist texts and teachings. That much of the nobility obstinately defended the custom, however, was to their great collective detriment. Internationally, polygamy was viewed as a symbol of Siamese backwardness. Its persistence provided colonial powers with an excuse to impose highly unequal treaty provisions and, potentially, deprive the country of its independence should France or Britain have elected to carry the white man's burden into Siam.[8] In addition, as the absolute monarchy began to run afoul of an increasingly vociferous, modernized middle class in Bangkok, polygamy figured prominently in the pointed derision of the nobility as a listless, profligate, lascivious holdover from an uncivilized time.[9] When disgust for the old order spread deeply enough into the bureaucracy and the military, it offered top officials the opportunity to seize power and abolish the absolute monarchy in June 1932.

That Bangkok's bourgeoisie increasingly identified with liberal ideals of equality and freedom — and grounded their virtually unanimous condemnation of polygamy in Enlightenment ideas — did not mean they practiced monogamy themselves. In fact, it was precisely when the calls for legal reforms in matters of family law intensified that Thailand's sex industry exploded into a massive business. Legally sanctioned, officially licensed, and regularly taxed, prostitution

---

8. Loos, *Subject Siam*, Ch. 4.
9. Scot Barmé, *Woman, Man, Bangkok: Love, Sex, and Popular Culture in Thailand* (Chiang Mai: Silkworm Books, 2002), Ch. 6.

had been around for hundreds of years. But if it had experienced considerable growth in the nineteenth century, owing to the immigration of Chinese men who almost invariably left their women behind, it was the institution of a modern, salaried bureaucracy — and hence the creation of an upper-middle class — that infused loads of freshly minted cash into the trade. In the early twentieth century, brothels became Bangkok's main claim to fame. Streetwalkers appeared all over town. And the erotic shows precursors to those that now attract throngs of tourists to Patpong — where ugly women use mangled vaginas to smoke cigarettes, play the trumpet, or shoot darts into balloons fifteen feet away — became a staple of the city's famed nightlife.[10] Modernization may well enlighten minds, but whose cock has ever read Voltaire?

For the women, the motivation to staff brothels was much the same back then as it is today. Among the tiniest of the millions-strong masses of *phu noi* ("little people"), there existed a long tradition of female participation in the labor force — much like today, women were often expected to work to feed their parents and their children. And if the economic life of the city offered women "with needs" a plethora of demeaning, exploitative careers, selling sex was often the most remunerative among them. Tens of thousands went for it willingly, if not eagerly. Many others had the decision made for them, as it was customary for parents to sell their teenage daughters into brothels should the need arise to pay off debts or otherwise cash out the proceeds of their investment on female offspring in a single lump sum.

The glaring dissonance between the reality of an exploding market for able-bodied women and the myth of a sexually conservative populace, now further enlightened by a newfound sense of national identity, individual freedom, and equality, was patched up with the same glue that precariously holds together every cultural system humans ever devised. The solution was an immoderate dose of hypocrisy in the

---

10. Ibid., Ch. 3.

public debate about women and morality, as well as the enshrinement of said hypocrisy in the nation's legal apparatus.

In the face of the first, almost entirely homegrown boom at the turn of the twentieth century, the government's instinct was to profit from the trade — just as it did in premodern times, when brothels in Ayutthaya were registered, tax-paying businesses. And so brothel taxes, much like those levied on opium and gambling dens, began in earnest to fill the state's coffers — a contribution that was, however, attenuated by the countervailing determination of entrepreneurs and civil servants to profit from the trade at the government's expense. With the complicity of police and high-ranking civil servants, many a self-respecting brothel owner took his business underground. On the one hand, owners merely sought to maximize profits — then as now, bribes were cheaper than taxes. On the other hand, they sought to minimize the risk that their businesses would be shut down should too many of their workers be found to be afflicted by venereal diseases. Characteristically, the main impediment to the enforcement of the law was that the interests of the state diverged from those of the state's officialdom. So while the sex scene thrived throughout much of the city, it did so largely outside the government's control.

It took about a half century before the Thai government could devise a clever policy that would benefit businessmen and civil servants as well as the state. At first, Sarit Thanarat's authoritarian regime banned prostitution outright. The ban was only partially relaxed in 1966, so to this day the practice remains technically illegal. Subsequently, the Vietnam War and the influx of dollar-bearing American soldiers caused the demand for pretty young women to skyrocket — multiplying profit-making opportunities for police officers, state officials, and businesspeople — and induced policymakers to look the other way so as not to compromise the torrent of economic aid that good US-Thai relations guaranteed. At the end of the war, the departure of US troops threatened to bring the whole party to a sudden, screeching halt. But that was never going to happen.

The government figured that the same infrastructure of hotels, restaurants, bars, and brothels that had made American servicemen so comfortable in Thailand could accommodate scores of restless Western warriors who had no wars to fight — that is, if they only knew about the laxity of the country's laws, the submissiveness of its people, and the looseness of its women. It is at this point that the Thai government began to promote tourism — "Welcome to the Land of Smiles!" — by portraying its women as eager to satisfy a visitor's every desire, and its population at large as a mass of slobbering fools eager to share wives, husbands, brothers, sisters, sons, and daughters, all the while smiling meekly, with any white man so kind as to spare a few bucks. The results were spectacular. Some studies suggest that the influx of foreign tourists grew from a paltry forty thousand in the late 1950s to a staggering twelve million visitors forty years on.[11] The beauty is that everyone who matters benefits. Brothel owners prosper. The police has a steady source of revenue to compensate for its chronic underfunding. Legitimate businesses flourish as sideshows around the main attraction — lining in gold the pockets of many an aristocrat, state official, and army general. And the remittances that flow copiously from Bangkok to the countryside have long kept taxes low for the emerging Thai bourgeoisie.

Despite the undeniable contribution they have made to the prosperity of the country, the tens of thousands of provincial girls whom foreigners assiduously patronize in the dazzling number of brothels, massage parlors, and bars operating in Bangkok and elsewhere are typically looked upon with distaste — especially by those urban, upper-middle-class Thais who most profit from their work. A common approach is sim-

---

11. Chris Baker and Pasuk Phongpaichit, *A History of Thailand* (New York: Cambridge University Press, 2005), p. 149 and p. 204; see also Jeffrey, *Sex and Borders*, p. 78.

ply to pretend they do not exist. Even as the country was being transformed by its rulers into a whorehouse — a veritable beggars' banquet — the Thai press spent much of the past century nostalgically lamenting the decline of Thai culture reflected in the far too revealing outfits now worn by city girls, the far too suggestive dances they can be observed performing in local discos, and the far too evident loss of propriety exhibited by teenagers who openly date their classmates in the absence of a formally proffered, carefully pondered, and solemnly approved marriage proposal. For anyone who has ever spent any time in Bangkok, to read the ongoing debates on morality and sex in the editorial pages of Thai English-language newspapers is to venture into a parallel universe — a bourgeois black hole disconnected from the everyday reality of Bangkok's busy streets.

In those pages, one can find stern condemnations of "Coyote dancing," a practice performed by bartenders in nightclubs that threatens irreparably to corrupt the city's youth. Or one can find discussions raging on about the merits of the government-imposed ban on pornographic websites. All websites found to include obscene content are blocked by the ever-blundering Ministry of Information and Communication Technology — a fancy name for Ministry of Propaganda, whose most insidious aspirations are undermined by the comical incompetence proper to every government agency in Thailand. Laughably swept under the rug is the shrill dissonance between the government's ongoing moral crusade and the fact that even the most depraved acts featured on the World Wide Web are offered by scores of local women to anyone in Bangkok with the means to afford an internet connection.

The government's hypocrisy on matters of sex and prostitution has risen to new, dizzying heights during the premiership of Abhisit Vejjajiva. Upon learning that cash-strapped, if notoriously consumption-conscious college students in Bangkok have increasingly taken to advertising sexual services on social networking sites, the government feigned alarm, indignation, and grave concern over the threat posed by the practice to the morality of the city's youth and the integrity of the country's social fabric. As if to highlight the severity of this gathering danger to Thai society, it was the current Prime Minister himself who took the time personally to reassure the country's bourgeoisie that the government would swiftly intervene — cracking down with the usual mixture of censorship and wasteful re-education campaigns aimed at teaching students the "right values."[12] It is anyone's guess, really, where teenagers in Bangkok would have learned the "wrong" values. Most probably, it was their growing exposure to Western culture and media that tragically led them astray.

In a country where tens of thousands of young women — possibly as many as several hundreds of thousands[13] — copulate for a living, one might ask what is the point of imposing a ban of internet pornography, of lamenting the dangers of pre-marital sex, or of expressing alarm over a handful of students who screw their classmates to finance their weekend shopping. And if modesty, chastity, and innocence are so important to the idea of "Thainess" (*kwam pen thai*), it may baffle some that purists and cultural warriors would spend so much time fending off comparatively small threats to that ideal. What many foreigners do not understand, however, is that the filthy whores who have spent decades fueling the nation's growth, keeping entire villages afloat, and filling to the brim the coffers of the state simply do not count. Nor do the large numbers of provincial women in Bangkok — whatever their day job happens to be — who are well known to be available for liaisons involving some, if perhaps less direct form of cash payment.

For the smug bourgeoisie, whose broken English is just

---

12. "PM Tells ICT to Crack Down on Prostitution Portal Websites," *The Nation* (Online Breaking News), February 2, 2009.
13. Jeffrey, *Sex and Borders*, p. 78; Pasuk, Sungsidh, and Nualnoi, *Guns, Girls, Gambling, Ganja*, pp. 196-208.

good enough to read brain-dead editorials in the *Bangkok Post* or *The Nation*, the provincial girls who live in Bangkok are not really citizens of Thailand — not the same way they are. These women, after all, belong to a social class whose sole prerogative, in the heinous cosmology of the *phu yai* ("big man"), is to grovel. Their duty is not merely to be poor — if not so poor as to inconvenience the highest authorities of the state into making token gestures of support — but rather to be content with the prospect of forever remaining poor.

At least since the dictatorship of Sarit Thanarat, the notion that the provincial masses belong in the fields, that they should not take part in materialistic pursuits on the streets of the capital city, has been a centerpiece of Thailand's official ideology. So economic migrants to Bangkok, especially those whose unsightly occupations reflect poorly on the country's leadership, have long been treated as outcasts — their insolence and stubborn refusal to embrace their station in life threatening the "deterioration" of Thai culture and society.[14] As such, debates in the Thai media focus almost exclusively on the sexual mores of middle- or upper-class city girls — and, occasionally, the peasant women who are still expected to serve as a symbol of cultural purity for the comfort of the Bangkok elites. The ubiquitousness of the sex industry in Bangkok is not inconsistent with the elites' image of Thailand as a sexually demure, conservative country. Nor, for that matter, does it undermine their self-appointed role as the upholders of that myth. The army of streetwalkers, go-go dancers, and tentacled masseuses working in Bangkok, then, are not commonly regarded as the long-lost daughters whom the double-breasted, uniformed, and garishly bejeweled fathers of the nation have sold into prostitution. Far from being gratefully acknowledged for the heroic contribution they have made to the country's prosperity, they are rather more conveniently ignored.

---

14. See Thak, *Thailand: The Politics of Despotic Paternalism*, pp. 105-106 and p. 122.

When their existence is acknowledged, the girls are treated with considerable ambivalence. On the one hand, as the country has grown synonymous with cheap and easy sex, they have been portrayed as quintessentially un-Thai — a category wholly distinct from the altogether more modest, more virtuous women of the same age who just happen to live off their parents' wealth or have found more reputable (if perhaps less gainful) employment. In this narrative, prostitutes are scapegoated as the loafing, conniving reprobates responsible for giving the country a bad name. They are a scourge, an indelible stain on the image of Thailand around the world — that which enables the fiendish white man to further weaken the country with the intent to rape and pillage it more freely still. Incidentally, the increased self-consciousness exhibited by the Thai leadership about the country's reputation has produced very positive results. In the 1990s, for instance, Thailand launched a remarkably successful campaign to eradicate HIV/AIDS and destroy any trace of (visible) child prostitution. Once reportedly ubiquitous in Bangkok's red-light districts, the practice is now banished behind the walls of dingy brothels that serve, discreetly, the needs of Thai men.

On the other hand, at times the prostitute is used as a metaphor for Thailand itself — a country whose blissful, bucolic innocence has forever been lost to the white man's overbearing, foam-at-the-mouth rapaciousness. To be clear, as a matter of personal choice it is certainly the case that prostitution is born of the lack of economic opportunity. In this sense, those who see Thailand as the hapless victim of the rigged system of globalized capitalism may be right to trace its women's lack of opportunity to the subordinate position to which Thailand is relegated on the world stage. It is also the case that in spite of the economic boom the country has experienced over the past thirty years, its largely rural population has suffered from international competition. Their goods have gotten cheaper, their daughters more readily available. But who exactly is responsible for pimping Thailand's provincial youth? Who, if not the country's self-styled paternalistic leadership? And why, if not for the benefit of the urban elites? This nativist reasoning conveniently ignores the fact that the transformation of Thailand into the West's playroom was conscious and deliberate, motivated by the opportunity for massive financial gain it presented to those who had *already* been blessed with riches and power — politicians, generals, the royal family, and their benefactors in the business community. And it neglects to consider how it benefits the high-minded bourgeoisie, who can go about their business without wasting too much time thinking about exporting a measure of economic opportunity to the provinces.

If, as the People's Alliance for Democracy so often lamented, Thailand is really up "for sale," who exactly is selling the country away? At least on this count, it certainly was not Thaksin or his minions. It was rather the same kind of royalist, unelected military government the PAD most recently sought to restore that transformed vast swaths of this proud country into a degenerate open-air bordello. Incidentally, these are the same military leaders who sold off entire sectors of Thailand's economy to foreign and domestic oligopolists, in exchange for billions of dollars paid on the condition that the generals make life difficult for smaller, local competitors and that they repress any labor movement that might seek better pay and work conditions for millions of Thai workers.[15] All of this for the economic benefit, and with the enthusiastic support, of the very social class that forms the hard core of the PAD's base. At the end of the day, who owns the hotels, the shopping malls, and massage parlors that foreign tourists and rich locals patronize? Who leases the land, lends the capital, supplies the construction materials, and oversees the building of mega-projects in popular tourist destinations? And who sells the ugly Westerner the beer he drinks, the food he eats, the condoms he wears, the cigarettes he smokes, and the souvenirs he brings home as evidence he did not spend

---

15. See Akira, *Capital Accumulation in Thailand*, pp. 179-180.

his entire trip holed up in a brothel?

Follow the money. For every miscreant who descends upon Thailand, weighted down by the oversized baggage of smug condescension Westerners carry with them everywhere they go, there are scores of enablers who benefit from the trade. They have a deal, you see. It is an unspoken one, but as ironclad as any contract one could ever sign in this country. And, thus far, successive generations have seen it fit to honor it. All the conservative, urbane elites are asked to do is refrain from making too big a fuss about the wide availability of plebeian girls. So long as they do not do a damn thing about it, in return they get to publicly berate the white man's shocking degeneracy, to bemoan his influence on the ignorant, impressionable little people, and thus proudly to wear the mantle of strenuous defenders of Thailand's national identity. All the while, behind closed doors, millions of their own men engage in much the same behavior.

It is in this light that one should read the recent, if now effectively defunct debate over the legalization of prostitution in Thailand. It is questionable whether Western sex tourists have much to gain from the decriminalization of the trade or its increased regulation. Prostitutes could hardly be more widely or more openly available. At the same time, in an effort to keep the authorities' attention elsewhere, most go-go bars and brothels patronized by Western tourists have, on their own initiative, taken aggressive steps to make the girls disease-free. In all but the cheapest, filthiest establishments, each "entertainer" and "special service" girl submits to monthly HIV tests and regular gynecological inspections.

Legalization, in this sense, would change only one thing. The licensing and registration requirements would put an official imprimatur on today's much disputed, unofficial estimates, thus bursting the illusion nurtured by those in the elites who still claim Thailand to be a sexually modest, conservative country. The fact that all that would then be allowed to happen legally, on the watch of the feudal aristocracy and the self-righteous bourgeoisie, would expose these groups as co-responsible for the phenomenon — knocking them off the pedestal of stalwart cultural guardians to which they have long elevated themselves. Unsurprisingly, the opposition to the proposal that Thailand allow de jure what has de facto been encouraged for decades was framed precisely around the need to defend Thainess and its values — as if to formally prohibit something one is informally peddling would do anything to affirm Thai morality. Then again, that was the whole point. So long as it is not enforced, the law as it stands has no adverse effect on tourism revenue streams. The veneer of cultural purism coming at no cost whatsoever, there is no point being seen wallowing in feces with all manners of Western swine.

For Thailand's royalist establishment, the great thing about the status quo — beyond the fact that tourism makes businesses more prosperous, jobs more remunerative, and taxes less burdensome — is that while the measly sums families upcountry receive from their daughters keep them afloat and hence muffle the clamor for a more interventionist role of the state, in the absence of real economic development millions of provincial bores never go far beyond mere subsistence. Incidentally, though "economic sufficiency" is all His Majesty the King and his toadies say provincial Thais should aspire to, the continuing reality of rural poverty perpetuates the incentive structure that makes prostitution the best possible career choice for upcountry girls by the hundreds of thousands. You can force people into mere "sufficiency," but it is quite another thing to extinguish any yearning for self-advancement, to sear upon people's faces idiotic smiles of contentment. Nor, for that matter, would Bangkok's elites really want for the slogging proles to surrender all hopes of a better life — not lest they piss away the steady supply of cheap labor that makes their useless, parasitic lives so comfortable.

Even the humblest Party member is expected to be competent, industrious and even intelligent within narrow limits, but it is also necessary that he should be a credulous and ignorant fanatic whose prevailing moods are fear, hatred, adulation and orgiastic triumph.

—GEORGE ORWELL
Nineteen Eighty-Four

FIVE

DEMOCRACY THAI STYLE

> Siam and Europe have taken very different historical courses. Therefore, it is totally mistaken to try to introduce Western ideas as they are. We cannot cultivate rice in Siam using European agricultural textbooks about wheat. Western political institutions, such as parliaments or political parties, are not suitable for Siam where the king traditionally leads a backward population.
>
> —King Chulalongkorn[1]

In 1903, King Chulalongkorn "the Great" reiterated thus his opposition to liberal-democratic reforms. Over a hundred years later, his words might appear self-serving enough. Chulalongkorn, after all, is the monarch who introduced European-style absolutism to Siam. He is celebrated as an enlightened ruler and a reformer for revolutionizing the Siamese public administration, for virtually abolishing slavery, for championing the study of science, for completely overhauling the country's legal and educational system, as well as for rationalizing the training, the life, and the teachings of

---

1. *The Royal Discourse on Unity*, cited in Eiji Murashima, "The Origin of Official State Ideology in Thailand," *Journal of Southeast Asian Studies* 19(1988): 80-96.

the *sangha*, the Buddhist monkhood. Ever an advocate of the "civilization" of Siam, on one thing Chulalongkorn was not willing to compromise: the unfetteredness of his own power. The same king who had embraced countless "Western" innovations to fulfill his vision of progress for Siam now denounced liberal-democratic ideas as un-Thai, incompatible with the country's traditions, and hence necessarily dangerous to the unity, stability, and prosperity of the nation.

Chulalongkorn has scores of disciples among lesser contemporary statesmen — dictators who routinely dismiss political competition, representative government, and the free exercise of a basic set of civil rights as much too Western, unsuited for their countries' unique histories and distinctive political traditions. From Vladimir Putin to General Musharraf, from Malaysia's Mahatir Mohamad to Burma's Than Shwe, despots the world over have chosen to hide behind the thick smokescreen of cultural distinctiveness to justify their autocratic rule and assert the prudence of proceeding with deliberation — if at all — in the implementation of even the most limited of democratic reforms. Why this line of reasoning is so popular among self-styled paternalistic rulers is apparent. In contemporary political discourse, "culture" is the only word whose international currency rivals democracy's. To be sure, culture commands more respect than the "dictatorship" and "oppression" it is frequently called upon to mask.

Back home, the culture-based argument against democracy can be made to fit almost any story about the content of national identities and almost any narrative about the imperative to protect traditional values from corrupting alien impositions. *Presto!* Kings, ayatollahs, generals, and tin-pots of all colors and stripes have at their disposal a highly portable piece of rhetorical chicanery to spiritualize their rule, identify their personal interests with those of the nation, and elevate themselves to the role of protector — indeed, possibly the very embodiment — of a rich cultural heritage and time-honored political traditions.

Better still, the argument appeals to a variegated Western constituency numbering conservatives and progressives alike. In some, it evokes the long-standing suspicion that non-Western populations are decidedly unfit for democracy, on account of both their backwardness and the obscurantism of their cultures. John Stuart Mill articulated such a position quite eloquently when he argued that "despotism is a legitimate mode of government in dealing with barbarians."[2] In this respect, at least, Chulalongkorn was quite right not to regard liberal reforms as of great expediency as he sought to avert the kind of colonial overlordship that had successively befallen each of the country's neighbors. In 1885, eleven members of the Siamese elite studying abroad had advised him to move gradually in the direction of constitutional monarchy — in their opinion, liberal reforms would have defused the threat of French and British colonization by rendering Siam more respected as a civilized nation in the eyes of the Europeans.[3] It is likely, however, that neither Britain nor France would have been impressed with the introduction of democratic reforms in a place like Siam, whose population at the time was widely considered "at best semi-barbarous."[4]

Nowadays, Mill's position is seldom reaffirmed with either the vehemence or the rhetorical flourish of nineteenth century writers, but it still holds considerable sway over Western thought and public opinion. Whether economic modernization is indeed a pre-condition for the success of democracy has been the subject of a lively debate over the past decades — a market economy, economic development, and high levels of education often being cited as pre-requisites.[5] And the

---

2. John Stuart Mill, *On Liberty* (New York: Macmillan, 1956[1869]), p. 14.
3. Murashima, "The Origin of Official State Ideology," p. 84.
4. These are the words of F.A. Neale, whose unflattering characterization of the Siamese people is echoed by many of his contemporary Western observers. See, for instance, Baker and Pasuk, *A History of Thailand*, p. 40.
5. See, for instance, Seymour Martin Lipset, "Some Prerequisites

existence of grave cultural impediments to the diffusion of democratic values to non-Western societies has been argued most famously in Samuel Huntington's *Clash of Civilizations*.[6] Huntington contends for the rootedness of democratic ideals in the values of tolerance, secularism, and individual autonomy unique to the Western, Judeo-Christian civilization. The prospects of democratic consolidation are said to be much bleaker in non-Western societies. The authoritarian, hierarchical, and collectivist nature of their cultures, in fact, renders most other "civilizations" eminently ill-suited for the internalization of democratic values.

Somewhat improbably, arguments along the lines of King Chulalongkorn's have also struck a chord with portions of the Western political left — self-loathing Westerners whom third world dictators have somehow turned into their apologists, useful idiots persuaded not only that basic human rights are, indeed, "alienable" but also that championing the right of non-Western peoples to speak their minds and otherwise control their own destiny amounts to doing violence to their cultural heritage. Never mind that concepts such as "Asian values" or *kwam pen thai* are invariably murky, ill-defined, selectively substantiated, and very much amenable to competing interpretations. And never mind that, unsurprisingly, indigenous perspectives on the compatibility of democracy with local cultural norms can hardly be abstracted from the interests of parties embroiled in bitter fights for political power.

The blind acceptance of the authorities' own version of what is compatible with a country's distinctive political traditions plays right into the hands of rulers who — as any *pater familias* worth his salt no doubt would — arrogate the authority to define what national identities are really about

---

of Democracy: Economic Development and Political Legitimacy," *American Political Science Review* 53(1959): 69-105.
6. Samuel P. Huntington, *The Clash of Civilizations and the Remaking of the World Order* (New York: Simon & Schuster, 1998).

and command the persuasive/coercive apparatus to shove their official ideologies down an entire population's throat. Democracy is then demeaned as another Western "imposition" on venerable non-Western cultures, which are thereby implicitly assumed never to have contemplated such abstruse ideas as tolerance, individual rights, and political participation. The end result is paradoxical indeed: the belief in the equal worth and respectability of all cultures is transformed — through the trivialization of the complexity of those very cultural systems — into an apology of dictators who often have little sympathy for cultural minorities, little time for opinions contrary to their own, and little patience for the plight of their own people.

In Thailand, of course, the word "democracy" has been a centerpiece of the state's official ideology since the absolute monarchy was toppled in 1932.[7] Still, authoritarian rulers from Sarit on down have long asserted the irrelevance of supposedly Western standards — invoking the amorphous concept of "Thai-Style" Democracy as an alternative better suited to Thailand's history, values, and traditions. To be clear, the "Thai-Style" in "Thai-Style Democracy" speaks to the restrictions that should be placed on both the freedoms enjoyed by the country's citizens and the autonomy exercised by its elected officials.

The idea of Thai-Style Democracy first surfaced in the late 1950s, as a post-hoc rationalization for Field Marshal Sarit Thanarat's conservative "revolution," and then as the ideological underpinnings of his manifestly undemocratic rule. Its basic principles were not entirely new, but rather echoed the political thought sketched out in well-known writings by King Vajiravudh (r. 1910-1925), Prince Dhani Nivas, and Luang Wichit Wathakan.[8] In 1957, Sarit had overthrown the long-

---

7. See Michael K. Connors, *Democracy and National Identity in Thailand* (Copenhagen: NIAS Press, 2007).
8. For a taste of King Vajiravudh's ideas on the subject, see Scot Barmé, *Luang Wichit Wathakan and the Creation of a Thai Iden-*

serving Prime Minister, Field Marshal Phibul Songkhram. As his own *Cremation Volume* recounts it, however, months after the coup Sarit remained deeply dissatisfied over the fact that "there still existed a parliament, political parties, a free press system that could criticize the government," and "labor unions that could go on strike whenever they were unhappy with their employers;" in spite of its best efforts, the government could not "do its work properly" under such trying circumstances.[9] Shortly thereafter, Sarit staged an *autogolpe* that dispensed with these features of "Western-style democracy" — installing a dictatorial regime supposedly more compatible with Thailand's political culture and more appropriate to the country's status as a developing nation.

Political rights like freedom of speech and association, as well as recurrent legislative elections, were scrapped in favor of a style of "representation" by which the father-leader (*pho khun*) would visit his "children" around the country, listen to their concerns, and suitably reinterpret their demands. Civil liberties like those that guaranteed criminal defendants a measure of due process were abandoned in favor of provisions like Article 17 of the 1959 constitution, which allowed the Prime Minister to order the execution without trial of anyone he deemed a threat to national security. The monarchy was resurrected as a source of legitimacy, a symbol of national unity, and a "moral check and balance" on the country's government. And the ideal of equality championed by some People's Party politicians like Pridi Banomyong was superseded by the government's unabashed attempt to entrench existing inequalities. The country's most powerful domestic capitalists were nurtured by the state and protected from competition, while top military and civilian leaders were al-

---

tity (Singapore: Institute of Southeast Asian Studies, 1993), pp. 30-31. A good summary of Prince Dhani's thought appears in Paul M. Handley, *The King Never Smiles* (New Haven: Yale University Press, 2006), pp. 84-86.

9. Cited in Thak, *Thailand: The Politics of Despotic Paternalism*, p. 95.

lowed to get rich by raiding the state's treasury. Meanwhile, the government repressed the demands of labor and insisted that the rural population should be forever content to eke out a simple existence upcountry.[10]

To be sure, Sarit has been dead for almost a half century. And, thanks to the sacrifice made by the bravest among them, the good people of Thailand were granted at least formal recognition for many of the political rights and civil liberties Sarit reckoned they did not deserve. Yet, "Thai-Style Democracy" (and its awkward contemporary variant, "democracy with the King as head of state"[11]) is still the cornerstone of Thailand's official ideology. The monarchy remains inviolate and immune from even the most benign criticism. Unelected institutions can still impose their will on the people's representatives; when elected politicians refuse to play along, they are accused of being "corrupt," "immoral," and hence worthy of removal via coups d'état promptly endorsed by His Majesty the King.[12] Sarit, moreover, remains the patron saint of the Thai elites. Having conveniently forgotten the fact that the great dictator pocketed public funds to the tune of billions of baht, elite writers still long, with poetic nostalgia, for the order, stability, and social harmony that Sarit guaranteed by keeping the little people in their place.[13]

Most recently, it is in this well-established school of thought that the People's Alliance for Democracy sought to ground its calls for a "New Politics" — the kind of politics that

---

10. For a concise overview, see Kevin Hewison, "Crafting Thailand's New Social Contract," *The Pacific Review*, 17(2004): 503-522. See also Kevin Hewison, "Thai-Style Democracy: A Conservative Struggle for Thailand's Politics," Paper presented at the Faculty of Political Science of Chulalongkorn University on June 26, 2009.
11. Connors, *Democracy and National Identity*, pp. 135-142.
12. For a contemporary apology, see Pattana Kitiarsa, "In Defense of the Thai-Style Democracy," Asia Research Institute, National University of Singapore, October 12, 2006.
13. Pridiyathorn Devakula, "Missing Field Marshal Sarit and Professor Sanya, I Am," *The Nation*, January 5, 2009.

would roll back the democratic reforms haphazardly implemented over the past half-century in favor of a form of government fit to provide Thailand's uneducated, dispossessed masses the requisite protection and guidance. Implicit in the PAD's message was, once again, the idea that the freedoms of thought, speech, and association democracy provides, as well as the power its vests in elected officials, are much too steeped in Western history and culture to be of any practical use in non-Western settings.

That "Thai-Style democracy," with the oversized role it has historically conferred upon unelected institutions, would amount to little more than a bastardization should be transparent enough by now. Perhaps less obvious is the notion that, in principle as well as in practice, "Thai-Style Democracy" has even less to do with Thai culture than it has with democracy. In this sense, advocates of democratization tend to defer much too readily to the sniveling apologists of the current regime on the true content of Thai culture. And those fancying themselves the proud defenders of Thailand's cultural heritage — that is, those for whom cultural discourse is more than a cheap trick to justify a privileged elite's monopolization of power — often betray a rather cartoonish view of both the "culture" they seek to defend and the alien cultures whose encroachments they so stalwartly oppose.

Notwithstanding the lip service frequently paid to the customs, practices, values, norms, and beliefs that cumulated over centuries of Thai political development, there is nothing "Thai" about lining up dissidents against the wall of a Buddhist temple and mowing them down with machine guns. There is nothing "Thai" about the shameless hypocrisy required to praise a military dictator who stole billions and murdered hundreds, with the blessing of the country's highest authorities, and in the same breath adduce "corruption" and "human rights violations" as justification for staging military coups against elected leaders guilty of a fraction of those offenses. There is nothing "Thai" about turning religion into an instrument of political legitimacy. There is nothing "Thai" about cults of personality. There is nothing "Thai" about the enlistment of mass media and schools in the dissemination of propaganda. And there is nothing "Thai" about repressing the poor to benefit the rich. These are not the hallmarks of culture, Thai or otherwise. These are rather the attributes of authoritarianism — the main features of which were pioneered, for the most part, by generations of Western dictators.

The idiocy of juxtaposing "Thai culture" and "Western values" is perhaps most readily apparent in the debate raging on in the local and international press about the inadequate protection that Thailand affords to the expression of political views critical of the state's carefully crafted, jealously guarded, and systematically propagated official ideology. The most obvious sticking point on this count is the obscurantist lèse majesté legislation (Article 112 of the Criminal Code), whose violators are more zealously prosecuted and harshly punished today than at any point over the past hundred years.[14] The recent arrest, legal harassment, prosecution, and in some cases the imprisonment of politicians (e.g., Jakrapob Penkair — case pending, fugitive), pro-democracy activists (e.g., Darunee Charnchoensilpakul — multiple counts, sentenced to eighteen years in prison), novelists (e.g., Harry Nicolaides — sentenced to three years, since pardoned by the King), journalists (e.g., the BBC's Jonathan Head — cases now dismissed), college professors (e.g., Chulalongkorn University's Giles Ji Ungpakorn — case pending, fugitive), and bloggers (e.g., Suwicha Thakhor — sentenced to ten years, since pardoned by the King) attests to an inescapable reality. Thailand is a country that takes political prisoners. It is a country where those who object to the way the state is organized go to jail. For three to fifteen years, possibly more if the government eventually passes legislation that has been

---

14. See David Streckfuss, *The Truth on Trial in Thailand: Defamation, Treason, and Lèse-Majesté* (London: Routledge, 2010).

proposed before.[15]

In Thailand, no one can safely criticize the monarchy — not in the intimacy of one's own family and circle of friends, much less in public. The government actively encourages its citizens to snitch on their neighbors. The law, moreover, compels the police to investigate any report, however flimsy or dubiously motivated, filed by any citizen. Of course, fear of appearing to condone this most abominable of crimes is strong enough motivation for a police officer to pursue the cases that land on his desk to the fullest extent of the law — even simple acts of civil disobedience such as failing to stand for the royal anthem and accompanying propaganda video ritually played at the cinema before every movie.[16] In turn, the media's unwillingness to report on the content of the offenses — for fear of either running afoul of the law or diminishing their royalist credentials — not only prevents any real debate about the legislation itself, but also leaves the population at large effectively unaware of the infractions for which people are going to jail.

In a move that brings to mind the institution of the "Bocche per le denunzie segrete," the stone-carved lion's mouths where any citizen in the old Republic of Venice (697-1797 CE) could drop secret missives accusing neighbors and public officials of the most disparate offenses, the Thai government set up websites encouraging the public to report any comment, picture, video, or story on the World Wide Web critical of His Majesty the King or the monarchy.[17] The anonymous reports

---

15. Manop Thip-Osod and Kultida Samabuddhi, "Criminal Law Change Withdrawn," *Bangkok Post*, October 10, 2007.
16. "Moviegoer Faces Prison For Sitting During Anthem," *New York Times*, April 24, 2008.
17. The first such website, "protecttheking.net" (see "Thai Website to Protect the Monarchy," *BBC News*, February 5, 2009) is now defunct, owing to the government's failure to renew its domain registration (see "Official Forgot to Relist Protecttheking Site," *Bangkok Post*, December 7, 2009.). The Ministry of Communication and Information Technology, however, operates a similar webpage at

are then used to either initiate prosecutions or block access to thousands of internet pages. In flagrant violation of the law, most such websites are blocked by the Ministry of Information and Communication Technology without a court order.[18]

Stock defenses of lèse majesté are grounded, by turns, in the exceptionalism and unexceptionalism of Thailand's "democracy."[19] Some argue that there's really nothing special about the way Thailand protects the institution of the monarchy — that the infamous provisions in the country's Criminal Code are no different from the regulation of political speech commonplace in the most democratic of nations. It is often noted, in particular, that many countries typically described as democracies have laws that protect heads of state from vilification. In most such countries, however, the laws in question do not protect heads of state from criticism of the kind leveled by Ji Ungpakorn or Jonathan Head — mere descriptions, accurate or not, of the role they allege the monarchy has played in Thai politics — but only from slander and name-calling. Nor do such laws extend to the criticism of policies such as the royally-endorsed idea of the "sufficiency economy." Nor do they apply to works of fiction like Harry Nicolaides' — writings of the kind that Geoffrey Chaucer could get away with in fourteenth century England.

To make matters worse, whereas in most democratic countries someone accused of defaming a public figure must be shown to have more or less intentionally disseminated falsehoods or distorted the truth, it is well-established legal precedent in Thailand that the truth of one's statements, their grounding in fact, is not a defense in lèse majesté pros-

---

http://www.mict.go.th/re_complaint.php.
18. Frank G. Anderson, "Thailand Starting to Resemble Burma," *UPI Asia*, February 6, 2009.
19. For a famous piece that argues both points, in a manner evocative of a crash-up derby, see Bowornsak Uwanno, "The Law of Inviolability in Thailand: Lese Majeste — A Distinctive Character of Thai Democracy amid the Global Democratic Movement," *Bangkok Post*, April 7, 2009.

ecutions.[20] The offense is therefore less akin to defamation than it is to Orwellian *crimethink*. The law does not merely prohibit the slander of the royal institution, but rather proscribes the very act of thinking ill of it. In an article gloating over Darunee Charnchoensilpakul's conviction, *The Nation*'s columnist Avudh Panananda characterized Darunee's offense as tarnishing "the reputation of Their Majesties with malicious intent to sway the crowds to lose their reverence and trust in the monarchy."[21] As Avudh describes it, the real crime is not slander or defamation, but the loss of the "reverence and trust" that Thai subjects (and, increasingly, foreigners) are expected to offer the institution no matter what the circumstances. Quite possibly, a statement's grounding in fact will only serve to make the crime more heinous, to the extent that it might pose a greater threat of turning others into thought criminals.

Sometimes, the notion that there is nothing out of the ordinary about the lèse majesté legislation is accompanied by the assertion, if not really much in the way of argument, that the laws protect "national security."[22] This is why, for instance, the government insists that the trials be held in secret.[23] Justice Minister Pirapan Salirathavibhaga recently argued that the lèse majesté legislation imposes restrictions on personal liberty akin to security screening protocols requiring passengers in the United States to remove their shoes and belts and walk through a metal detector before they can board a commercial flight. Said restrictions, then, are supposed to be acceptable in that they protect the security of the

---

20. See David Streckfuss, "Kings in the Age of Nations: The Paradox of Lese-Majeste as Political Crime in Thailand," *Comparative Studies in Society and History* 37(1995): 445-475.
21. Avudh Panananda, "Da Torpedo's Downfall a Warning to the Like-Minded," *The Nation*, September 1, 2009.
22. "Thailand Vows to Stem Tide Against Royals," *Reuters*, January 10, 2009.
23. Pravit Rojanaphruk, "Closed Door Lese Majeste Trial for Daranee Makes Lawyer Despair," *The Nation*, June 25, 2009.

population from the unspecified calamities that might befall the country if Thailand's highest political institutions were subjected to the same scrutiny they receive in, say, England. It goes without saying, however, that a country prohibiting the mere discussion of political reform can hardly be called a "democracy." Democracy, the real thing, is founded upon freedom of speech precisely because it is believed that citizens have a right to demand political, economic, and social change. And, of course, most in need of legal protection are those minority viewpoints that the majority of the population might resent.

Because the extraordinary protection that the country's legal code affords the monarchy finds no equivalent in any democratic nation, the case for Thailand's "democratic unexceptionalism" is laughable. As a result, the veritable army of propagandists and third-rate academics tasked with the public defense of lèse majesté frequently revert to arguing the opposite case. The legislation, that is, is often championed on the grounds that it embodies that which makes Thailand *different* from other countries — that special relationship between the Thai people and their kings which no foreigner can truly comprehend.[24] Thus, lèse majesté laws are characterized as the last line of defense protecting the institution that lies at the very heart of Thailand's exceptionalism — an institution besieged by enemies foreign and domestic eager to trample on the country's time-honored traditions in their long-standing quest to remake Thailand in the image of the West.

Alas, well-intentioned people on both sides of this debate have a tendency to ignore the fact that no "culture" is really specific enough to mandate a single regime type, a single form of government, or a single configuration of institutions. This is true of "Thai culture" as much as it is true of the miscellany of cultures crudely lumped together under

---

24. Thanong Khanthong, "Foreign Media Coverage of Our Crisis is Distorted," *The Nation*, December 12, 2008.

the all-encompassing "Western" label. Lest we forget, it is in the country with arguably the proudest republican tradition in Europe — France — that the model of royal absolutism originated. Indeed, it is from French-style absolutism that King Chulalongkorn borrowed heavily in his attempt to build the kind of modern state that Thailand still lacked in the mid-nineteenth century. Is republican government any more compatible with French culture than monarchical rule? To be sure, few would have argued as much in 1790.[25] The fact is that "French culture" prescribes neither. French culture has given rise to, and has in turn been re-shaped by, royalist and republican ideas alike.

Lest we forget, moreover, most places in Western Europe have lived under more or less absolute monarchs much longer than Thailand has — not to mention much longer than they themselves have been "democratic." Liberal democracy, in this sense, may indeed be a Western achievement. But it is certainly a recent accomplishment — one that marked a sharp break with an overwhelmingly authoritarian past, as opposed to a seamless extension of its distinctive political traditions. Democratization not only constitutes a very recent development in countries like Italy, Spain, Portugal, and Greece; as recently as four or five decades ago, it was common to suspect that democracy was destined to fail in countries distinguished by the "parochial" and "subject" political cultures prevalent in southern Europe. Participatory, pluralist institutions, it was thought, are unlikely to work properly in contexts where citizens are generally passive, uninvolved, and deferential to elites.[26] Interestingly, these are more or less the same arguments made in support of Thailand's supposed incompatibility with "Western" democracy.

Just as there is nothing innately "democratic" about West-

---

25. For an illustration, see Edmund Burke, *Reflections on the Revolution in France* (London: Penguin Classics, 1986[1790]).
26. Gabriel A. Almond and Sidney Verba, *The Civic Culture* (Boston, MA: Little, Brown and Company, 1965).

ern culture, it could be argued that Thai culture is not quite as unfriendly to so-called "Western" democracy as it is often made out to be. In this respect, there are at least two inconvenient facts undermining the notion that lèse majesté is the legal expression of values more integral to Thai culture than would be the unfettered expression of political ideas.

The first is that no such thing as Thailand existed, whether as a political entity or even merely as an idea, as recently as two centuries ago. Not only is present-day Thailand essentially a negative construct — it includes contiguous territories in mainland Southeast Asia left over from French and British colonization. Prior to the nineteenth century, the rulers in Ayutthaya and then Bangkok never really controlled much territory beyond the Chao Phraya basin, the country's eastern seaboard, and parts of the Malay peninsula. When they did come to administer what is now Thailand's upper north, deep south, and vast sections of the outer northeast, it was not by plebiscite or popular insurrection that these territories gave their allegiance to the King of Siam. It was rather by conquest and skillful political maneuvering that Siam prevailed. Parts of northern Thailand, for instance, were brought under Siamese control in exchange for bailing the Lanna rulers out of the debts they had incurred with European trading companies.

How much sense, then, does it really make to speak of a single Thai culture? How can whatever Thai national identity the people of Udon Thani, Chiang Mai, and Nakhorn Si Thammarat share be understood without reference to the homogeneity enforced by the authorities in Bangkok through sustained propaganda and a good deal of violence — not to mention the most careless disregard for the plentiful local customs that were stamped out in the name of cultural homogeneization? And how "natural," "sacred," or otherwise worthy of insulation from domestic debate — to say nothing of "foreign" ideas — should we presume that single, national identity to be?

The other fact that has escaped many on both sides of the debate is that the lèse majesté legislation as it is currently interpreted and enforced is not something that has existed in Thailand from time immemorial. In fact, at least with respect to the monarchy, the Thai press was measurably freer a century ago than it is today. For much of their (absolute) reign, King Vajiravudh (Rama VI) and King Prajadhipok (Rama VII) were subjected to vicious criticism and a good deal of ridicule by the local press. And though repression was intermittently applied, the Thai journalists of the time could afford to be much more than the neutered bunch of sycophants they have now become. By the standards of our obscurantist times, when restrained, almost apologetic articles in the *Economist* pass for mortal affront, the cartoons and editorials routinely printed in the pages of early twentieth century Thai newspapers are positively shocking.[27]

In a recent work on the subject, David Streckfuss describes the importance of Theravada Buddhist cosmology to the interpretation and usage of the lèse majesté laws since their introduction in 1900 — above all the belief that one's stock of accumulated merit, reflected in existing social status, correlates with the goodness of one's character, the purity of one's intentions, the completeness of one's understanding of "the truth," and the legitimacy of one's access to political power.[28] Streckfuss shows how the combination of a worldview well rooted in traditional beliefs with modern legislation borrowed from Europe laid the foundations for Thailand's subsequent evolution into a "defamation regime."

The traditional worldview that Streckfuss refers to, however, is hardly unique to Theravada Buddhism. Perhaps most famously, almost twenty-five centuries ago Plato proposed that the hierarchies of power necessary to the well-being of an ideal polity be justified on the basis of a "Noble Lie." For

---
27. For a number of especially compelling illustrations, see Barmé, *Woman, Man, Bangkok*.
28. See David Streckfuss, *The Truth on Trial in Thailand*.

the sake of social harmony and cohesion, that is, Plato suggested that men of status both high and low should be led to believe that one's station in life is determined by the kind of metal God used to create them — gold for aristocrats, silver for warriors, bronze and iron for farmers and laborers. Plato himself described this as an "old Phoenician tale."[29]

Up until the advent of modern conceptions of citizenship, in the seventeenth century, neo-Platonic ideas like "the great chain of being" or Edward Forset's analogy of "bodies natural and politic" legitimized the vast inequalities in power and wealth prevalent in Europe based on the existence of natural, God-ordained hierarchies of superior and inferior men. Failure of any member to "keep his place" and "perform his duties," threatened the "disorder of the parts," which in turn harbored anarchy and social disintegration.[30] Not unlike those who staged "Holy Men Revolts" in northeastern Siam in the early 1900s,[31] Puritans could only justify defying the English monarchy in the 1640s by manufacturing a narrative that specified circumstances in which one could legitimately challenge his natural superiors without precipitating society's destruction. Whether founded in Buddhist cosmology, platonism, or the "divine right of kings," the notion that hierarchies in power and wealth are both natural and good is the oldest lie in the history of human societies.

Beyond the selective and self-serving readings of history upon which they are often based — interpretations that, ironically, tend to be bought wholesale only by those who have little appreciation for the complexity of any such "culture" — cultural defenses of authoritarian provisions such as Thailand's lèse majesté laws tend to be fairly circuitous. In

---

29. This appears at the end of Book III of Plato's *Republic*, written around 380 BC.
30. See Michael Walzer, *The Revolution of the Saints: A Study in the Origins of Radical Politics* (Cambridge: Harvard University Press, 1982), p. 175. See also pp. 153-154 and pp. 171-174.
31. For a summary, see Somchai Phatharathananunth, *Civil Society and Democratization* (Copenhagen: NIAS Press, 2006), pp. 26-28.

particular, if it is the very sanctity of "culture" that confers legitimacy upon an institution like the Thai monarchy, one might reasonably ask the following: Given that every cultural system constantly undergoes some form of change, do we concede that the institution in question is legitimate only to the extent that it reflects a people's *current* worldview and *current* collective identity? And, if so, what to make of dissenting voices? On the one hand, if the institution is truly reflective of cultural values that remain so deep-seated that most people could not imagine dispensing with it, then dissenting views will be rejected by the population at large, with no damage done to either the country or its traditions. On the other hand, what if dissent reflects a real, ongoing cultural shift? Surely no "institution" would want to muzzle the expression of something so sacred as to justify its existence.

Either way, to repress dissent makes no sense — unless, that is, repression is needed to protect from corrupting alien influences the very cultural values that have supposedly caused the institution to come into being. Come to think of it, that might be the reason why Robert Mugabe, Than Shwe, or Vladimir Putin routinely brand their domestic opponents the instruments of foreign conspiracies — it makes repression not only justified, but crucial to the survival of the cultural heritage they ostensibly personify.

Generally speaking, however, political institutions are less about culture than they are about power. To be sure, the language and repertoire of values, rituals, and leadership styles that give every country's political life its unique, distinctive flavor is the product of that country's history — having characteristically evolved over a long period of time. But culture does not make social or political hierarchies. It is rather more often the case that hierarchy makes culture — or better, those legitimizing ideologies that the state habitually camouflages as culture. And, much like the "Thai-Style Democracy" it is designed to protect, lèse majesté as it is currently defined and enforced is neither "democratic" nor really all that "Thai." In point of fact, lèse majesté is but a quintessentially modern — and decidedly European — instrument of repression that twentieth century Thai dictators have weaponized to stifle political debate about the very content of Thai cultural values and identity. It exists not to defend Thai culture, but to enforce the cheapened, comic-book version of Thainess the members of the country's establishment have manufactured and propagated to advance no cause greater than their own aggrandizement.

Having elevated themselves to the role of protectors of the monarchy — in an attempt to legitimize their extra-constitutional, corrupt, violent rule — Thailand's ruling class has in lèse majesté a powerful instrument to defend its own hold on power. In fact, Thailand's lèse majesté legislation is less a mechanism to protect the monarchy than it is an instrument for the establishment to punish, harass, and muzzle its critics. Indeed, it is by design that the law is so open-ended, ambiguous, and susceptible to abuse. That anyone can file a complaint, that the definition of what constitutes injury to the monarchy is so expansive, that the incentive is strong for the police to pursue the pettiest of offenses, and that no accused can ever really mount a genuine defense — in court or the public square — is all to the great benefit of Thailand's ruling class of generals, aristocrats, and rich urbanites. So long as their actions are presumed to have the King's blessing, to have been undertaken in His Majesty's name, or at least to have been motivated by the desire to advance the interests of the monarchy, nobody can safely challenge the establishment without running the risk of being accused of either criticizing the monarchy or compromising its defense.[32]

Nobel laureate Amartya Sen famously argued that democratization does not equal Westernization.[33] Democracy

---

32. See, for an example, Don Sambandaraksa, "What Is Praise Worth When Criticism Is Forbidden?," *Bangkok Post*, September 30, 2009.
33. Amartya Sen, "Democracy and Its Global Roots: Why Democ-

has global roots — its seeds having been sown in the foundational texts and embedded social practices of a variety of cultures outside Western Europe. In Thailand, a frequently cited illustration is the venerable Ramkhamhaeng inscription (dated 1292 CE). At a time when most Westerners lived as serfs — essentially the property of feudal overlords — King Ramkhamhaeng of Sukhothai had these words inscribed on his throne:

> In the time of King Ramkhamhaeng this land of Sukhothai is thriving. There is fish in the water and rice in the fields. The lord of this realm does not levy toll on his subjects for traveling the roads; they lead their cattle to trade or ride their horses to sell; whoever wants to trade in elephants, does so; whoever wants to trade in horses, does so; whoever wants to trade in silver or gold, does so. [...] When commoners or men of rank differ and disagree, [the King] examines the case to get at the truth and settles it justly for them. He does not connive with thieves or favor concealers [of stolen goods]. When he sees someone's rice he does not covet it; when he sees someone's wealth he does not get angry. [...] When he captures enemy warriors, he does not kill them or beat them. He has hung a bell in the opening of the gate over there: if any commoner in the land has a grievance which sickens his belly and gripes his heart, and which he wants to make known to his ruler and lord, it is easy: he goes and strikes the bell which the King has hung there; King Ramkhamhaeng, the ruler of the kingdom, hears the call; he goes and questions the man, examines the case, and decides it justly for him. So the people of this *muang* of Sukhothai praise him.[34]

The Ramkhamhaeng inscription contrasts sharply with contemporary accounts of life in medieval Europe as well as with the model of political and social organization that

---

ratization is Not the Same as Westernization," *The New Republic*, October 6, 2003.

34. Translation in David K. Wyatt, *Studies in Thai History* (Chiang Mai: Silkworm Books, 1998), pp. 54-55.

became dominant in Siam with the rise of Ayutthaya. It describes a society ruled by an accessible king, one who is confident enough of his own position to routinely lower himself to the level of his subjects to adjudicate their disputes. The king is accorded praise and respect not simply *qua* inherently superior being, but because of what he does for his people. At the same time, the king's subjects are portrayed as remarkably equal under the law and free to pursue economic activities of their own choosing.

It may be doubtful whether life in Sukhothai was quite as idyllic as the inscription suggests — or whether, as conservative scholar Sulak Sivaraksa has claimed, Thai society really did embody the ideals of "liberty, equality, and fraternity" five hundred years before the French came up with that slogan.[35] Surely, Sukhothai cannot be described as "democratic" in the contemporary sense of the word.[36] Still, that Ramkhamhaeng would choose to eulogize his reign based on his commitment to individual freedom, equality before the law, government accountability, and the provision of services speaks to the centrality of these proto-democratic values to Thailand's cultural heritage. And although Ramkhamhaeng's explicit acknowledgment of liberal values does not make Thailand more ideally suited to democracy than any other country, the fact that these ideas have such deep roots in the country's history illustrates that there is nothing "unnatural" about some of democracy's most elemental principles. Indeed, the point is that no culture or civilization is inherently "friendly" or "unfriendly" to democracy. Its adoption, in Thailand and elsewhere, will invariably mark a departure from some established political traditions, and continuity with others — just

---

35. For some perspective on this subject, see radical Thai writer Jit Poumisak's *The Real Face of Thai Feudalism Today*, originally published under the pseudonym Somsamai Srisudravarna in 1957. In Craig J. Reynolds, *Thai Radical Discourse: The Real Face of Thai Feudalism Today* (Ithaca, NY: Southeast Asia Program, 1987), pp. 71-75.
36. For that matter, nor could Athens circa 500 BC.

like it did in the West, where it won out over more traditional, more oppressive forms of government through much blood, sweat, and tears.

This, incidentally, is as true of democracy as it is of every innovation that dictators are blithe to embrace if it furthers their own power or renders their lives more comfortable — from the plough or the wheel, all the way to a commercial agriculture, an industrial economy, a standing army, a centralized bureaucracy, a modern educational system, or the gold-plated sit-down toilets where they read the morning papers. Thailand is no exception. Prince Damrong Rajanubhab, the man known as the "father of Thai history," famously claimed that Thai culture is defined by its extraordinary ability to assimilate aspects of foreign cultures. With pride, Prince Damrong wrote: "The Tai knew how to pick and choose. When they saw some good feature in the culture of other people, if it was not in conflict with their own interests, they did not hesitate to borrow it and adapt it to their own requirements."[37] And so they did. Everything from *devaraja* rule to *sakdina*, from Theravada Buddhism to royal absolutism, from nationalist ideology to developmental policy was borrowed and adapted from abroad, such that the key organizing principles of modern Thai society are no less foreign than the Western "impositions" its elites now so vehemently resist.

Consider what are known today as the three pillars of "Thainess" — nation, religion, and king. Theravada Buddhism comes from Sri Lanka; its imposition from above, in the words of a well-known Thai scholar, "amounted to a direct historical assault on the local spirits of village and town."[38] Thai nationalism was fashioned during the reign of King Vajiravudh after European nationalism, just as the absolutist institutions his father introduced some decades earlier were cast in a European mold. And the concept of *devaraja* rule

---

37. Cited in Peleggi, *Thailand: The Worldly Kingdom*, p. 10.
38. Chatthip Nartsupha, *The Thai Village Economy in the Past* (Chiang Mai: Silkworm Books, 1999), p. 14.

— with its Brahmanical rituals, its mandated prostration, its rigid social hierarchy and exaltation of kings to the status of gods — was intentionally modeled by Ayutthaya's rulers after the great Khmer kingdoms of the time. Earlier on, historian David K. Wyatt suggests that King Ramkhamhaeng had self-consciously defined the administration of the Tai kingdom of Sukhothai in contrast to the more hierarchical, more unequal, more obsessively ritualistic Khmer kingdoms ruled by self-styled "gods."[39] And yet, with the rise of Ayutthaya, the Khmer practices Ramkhamhaeng deemed antithetical to Tai culture rapidly won out.

As Damrong noted, the only criterion that guided the introduction of these innovations — and countless others — was simply whether their adoption was "in the interest" of "the Tai." More plausibly, the real standard was the interest of those who happened to be in charge at the time. King Chulalongkorn himself, who questioned the wisdom of looking to European governments as models for Siam — something as ill-advised as it no doubt would be to "cultivate rice in Siam using European agricultural textbooks about wheat" — showed no such reservation when it came to organizing a bureaucracy that could raise his taxes and implement his decrees. On this count, the King was keen to defer to Western ideas: "The administration needs to rely upon the models set by Westerners who have acted upon them hundreds of times. We need people with a knowledge of Western administration to set a model for us."[40] Pre-existing local practices having posed no obstacle to innovations that advanced the interests of many a dictator, it is curious that they should be considered such a grave impediment to reforms that, at long last, promise to liberate and empower the people.

Culture may well be the first refuge of dictators. But it is important to recognize that "Thai-Style Democracy" does not

---
39. Wyatt, *Studies in Thai History*, p. 52.
40. Cited in Kullada Kesboonchoo Mead, *The Rise and Decline of Thai Absolutism* (New York: Routledge/Curzon, 2004), p. 68.

amount to anything more glamorous or exotic than your average European-style dictatorship. In fact, the real hindrance to democratization in Thailand is not Thai culture; it is rather the interest of elites who are otherwise eager to borrow from abroad what can be used to entrench their power at home. Accordingly, to reject democracy on cultural grounds is not to protect Thailand from Western impositions. It is rather to acknowledge the authority of pompous, inbred big men to define what is compatible with tradition and what is not. Beyond that, whether or not democracy is of any use to a country like Thailand remains very much a matter of taste. At the very least, though, there is nothing "un-Thai" about the freedom to control one's own destiny, to speak one's own mind, to form or join political organizations, to read materials other than a regime's propaganda, or to hold one's government accountable for its failures. Apparently, the hundreds of people murdered by the authorities in Thailand for their audacity to demand greater political rights were not fooled either. Purely as a matter of taste, I am rather more inclined to stand with them than their executioners.

Rebellion meant a look in the eyes, an inflection of the voice; at the most, an occasional whispered word. But the proles, if they could somehow become conscious of their own strength, would have no need to conspire. They needed only to rise up and shake themselves like a horse shaking off flies. If they chose they could blow the Party to pieces tomorrow morning. Surely sooner or later it must occur to them to do it? And yet—!

—GEORGE ORWELL
Nineteen Eighty-Four

SIX

REVOLT OF THE UNHOLY

> The sound of our cries, the cries of those who are worth only as much as the soil, the cries of those who were born on the land, and live on the land, will no doubt reach the sky. The Red Shirts want to say to the earth and the sky that we too have hearts. The Red Shirts want to remind the earth and the sky that we too are Thai. The Red Shirts want to ask the earth and the sky, if there is no rightful place for us here, are we to conquer for ourselves the space where we can firmly plant our feet?
>
> —Nattawut Saikua[1]

The good people of Thailand have a long history of meek acquiescence to coups d'état. So it was not altogether surprising that they appeared to breathe a collective sigh of relief when Abhisit Vejjajiva emerged from the siege of Suvarnabhumi and Don Muang with just enough votes in parliament to become Thailand's twenty-seventh Prime Minister. By-elections held on January 11, 2009 gave him an unexpected boost. The Democrat Party picked up a handful seats; its performance in a number of constituencies in northern and central Thailand

---

[1] Nattawut Saikua, "From the Earth to the Sky," speech given on December 30, 2008 (author's translation).

improved somewhat. The Thai people, it seemed, genuinely wanted the new government to succeed.

In fact, Thai voters had never quite warmed to Abhisit. Some sneered that this British-born, Oxford-educated son of privilege needed a visa to travel to the rural areas where most Thais still live. Despite his clean-cut, boyish looks, Abhisit is manifestly squirmy and uncomfortable in his own skin — his charisma and charm scarcely exceeding that expected of the greyest of bean-counters. Certainly, Barack Obama he is not. Still, having witnessed the People's Alliance for Democracy inflict untold damage on the Thai economy and the country's increasingly tenuous image around the world, many ordinary people were simply relieved when Thailand's royalist establishment executed the final stage of a carefully orchestrated plan — first, by using its control of the courts to remove a government that its military and paramilitary wings had mortally wounded through a mixture of disorder and insubordination; then, by forking out the cash needed to buy off a sufficient number of MPs to install their very own "nominee government." Precisely because of the elite support it enjoyed, Abhisit's government promised, at the very least, to return the country to a measure of normalcy. And, unlike the coterie of swine who have ruled Thailand for decades, the Thai people can be counted on to place country above partisan interest.

The filthy business of governing, however, was quick to expose Abhisit as the handsome face of another loathsome dictatorial regime. Barely a month into his ill-gotten term came the story of monstrous human rights abuses the Thai military had perpetrated on hundreds of Rohingya refugees, towed out to the high seas on barges equipped with no engines or sails, left to drown and starve to death.[2] As many as five hundred of them were still unaccounted for and presumed dead when the story broke. Then came the infuriating

---

2. Ishaan Tharoor, "Abandoned at Sea: The Sad Plight of the Rohingya," *Time*, January 18, 2009.

images, beamed into every television set around the world, of a young Australian man standing behind iron bars, weeping, chained and shackled for having written a novel no one had ever even bothered to read. It is not quite that, as the BBC's Jonathan Head speculated in the wake of the scandals,[3] these events signaled the end of Abhisit's honeymoon with the Thai people and the sleepier segments of the foreign press. After all, most Thais did not hold it against Thaksin when security forces murdered, in cold blood, dozens of Muslim demonstrators at Kru Ze and Tak Bai. Very few of them, moreover, would have lost any sleep over the fate of Harry Nicolaides.

The problem, then, was not just that Abhisit's crisp, white business shirt was now stained with Harry's tears and spatters of Rohingya blood. It was not just that Abhisit had graduated, in record time, to the rank of serial human rights abuser his patrons have long and somewhat proudly held. It was not just that Abhisit was an accessory to torture, murder, and the violation of the International Covenant on Civil and Political Rights — not to mention the acts of violence and treason that elevated him to the position he now occupied. The real problem was that it quickly became clear that Abhisit was eager to make apologies for the same practices he had vociferously denounced during Thaksin's tenure in office — in some cases, to make excuses for the very abuses that took place *during* Thaksin's administration.

Four years ago, we were told that Thaksin had to go because he bought votes and MPs. But the millions of baht each of Newin's "friends" received in exchange for joining Abhisit's coalition was an unmistakable sign of continuity with well-established practices — Newin did not somehow restore his virginity the moment he changed beds. We were told that Thaksin had to go because he wasted public resources to curry favor with low-income voters. But the new government's two-thousand-baht handout to ten million people, not to

---

3. Jonathan Head, "Honeymoon to Nightmare for Thai PM," *BBC News*, January 23, 2009.

mention the slew of populist proposals it swiftly devised,[4] were driven by electoral considerations at least as much as Thaksin's policies had been. We were told that Thaksin had to go because he silenced dissent. But Abhisit's administration quickly proceeded to muzzle its own opposition by launching a record-breaking number of prosecutions based on the country's barbarous lèse majesté laws[5] and the still more insidious Computer Crimes Act. We were told that Thaksin had to go because he abused human rights. But Abhisit did not hesitate to exculpate the military in the lurid Rohingya affair — all evidence to the contrary be damned. For good measure, the Prime Minister reached into Robert Mugabe's bag of tricks as he stonewalled the United Nations' attempt to gain access to the victims of his government's abuses,[6] accused eye-witnesses of hallucinating,[7] and then stoked xenophobic hatred by promising the Thai people he would strenuously defend the country from the hordes of (black) foreign invaders.[8]

A few short weeks was all it took to destroy the entire public case that Abhisit and his puppeteers had concocted to justify Thaksin's ouster. The catastrophic, shameful performance of Abhisit's cabinet made it clear that his cries for a cleaner, more honest government were a fraud — that Abhisit was neither serious about righting Thaksin's wrongs nor much inclined to meaningfully change course. In the process, the idea that Abhisit would ever be able to exercise power without the support of his current masters, from whom he might have ultimately hoped to extricate himself, appeared increasingly fanciful as the tragic charade continued to un-

---

4. "Reforms, Not Handouts," *Bangkok Post*, January 23, 2009.
5. See Marwaan Macan-Markar, "Thailand: Lese Majeste Cases Rise but Public in the Dark," Inter-Press Service, May 14, 2010.
6. Jonathan Head, "UN Awaits Thai Reply on Migrants," *BBC News*, January 23, 2009.
7. "PM: Rohingya Reports 'Exaggerated'," *Bangkok Post* (Online Breaking News), January 20, 2009.
8. "PM Vows Migrant Crackdown," *Bangkok Post* (Online Breaking News), January 22, 2009.

fold. Their crimes were now his own.

The corruption scandals that hit Abhisit's government, the atrocities it desperately sought to cover up, and the wave of repression it unleashed upon taking office quickly exposed Thailand's royalist establishment for all its hypocrisy. It was now evident that those who paralyzed the country and defaced Thailand's international image had gone to such extremes only just so they could replace the will of the people with their own, superior wisdom. Only just so they could substitute corrupt politicians inimical to their agenda with equally crooked but more malleable ones. Only just so they could establish their own dictatorship masqueraded in the most meaningless fripperies of democracy.

Safely ensconced behind their tanks, their guns, and their frenzied, *yah bah*-powered army of street thugs, the palace, the army, and parts of Bangkok's rapacious business community had, once again, destroyed the country's democratic institutions. To these groups, the people are mere beasts of burden, the producers of wealth they can plunder with impunity, the breeders of daughters they can sell into prostitution. For decades, the big men have told the people that they are too stupid, ignorant, and lazy to be entrusted with the destiny of the nation — that they have no business demanding the right to drive the entire country into the ground. For decades, they have branded anyone who dared challenge their right to use the state as personal pelf a traitor, a communist, a republican, or an agent of shadowy international conspiracies. And, for decades, they have smothered the people's aspirations in the blood of their bravest young men and women. Now they stood before the people, pressing a knife to their throat. It was their way or chaos, economic catastrophe, and civil war. Prostrate and crawl. Obey. Or else.

Of course, it is often the case that the darkest crises bear the most spectacular of possibilities. Thailand's predicament is no different. Indeed, dispiriting though it had been, the deranged journey that climaxed with Abhisit's rise to Prime

Minister recalled a rather more hopeful historical precedent. Back in 1991, in what was supposed to have been Thailand's last coup, the public had, at first, quietly acceded to military intervention — having been offered little reason to bemoan the ouster of a corrupt democratic government. Confronted with the obvious hypocrisy, corruption, and brutality of the new regime, the same urban middle classes who had applauded his rise to power forced Suchinda's shameful ouster in 1992.

It was at this painful juncture, then, after the decade of tragic setbacks that followed the triumph of the 1997 "People's Constitution," that the Thai people faced an unprecedented opportunity to take charge of their own destiny, to reach for what they had long been denied. As Thaksin's influence continued to wane, those committed to social and political change now had a chance to channel the unity of purpose the provincial masses had achieved under the leadership of Thai Rak Thai into a genuine democratic movement — one that could seek the people's empowerment but reject the corruption, the cronyism, the violence, and the contempt for the rule of law of the Thaksin era. At the same time, should Bangkok's students, professionals, and middle-income workers rise up — just as they did when they caught on to a similar fraud in 1992 — the possible alliance between the urban middle class and the once-dormant rural populace held historic promise for the country's prospects of democratization.

In some observers, the wave of demonstrations that shook Thailand during the Songkhran holidays, in April 2009, raised the hope that this kind of "people's revolution" was finally afoot. The demonstrations had started as a stunning success for the Red Shirts. The series of coordinated actions that led to the debacle in Pattaya — on April 11, hundreds of protesters commanded by former pop star Arisman Pongruangrong broke into the hotel where an ASEAN summit was taking place, forcing its cancellation and the hasty evacuation of foreign dignitaries — revealed an unexpected measure of discipline and organizational prowess for a movement often thought of as rudderless. The country's Prime Minister was humiliated and exposed as the puppet that he was — at once powerless to afford his illustrious guests the kind of security that civilized countries guarantee as a matter of course and so cowardly as to rely on a private armed militia, Newin Chidchob's "blue shirts," to ambush protesters he could not get the army or the police to keep out of the area.

When the military did step in, following the imposition of the emergency decree on April 12, even the incipient crackdown appeared to embolden the Red Shirts. The reaction of the authorities clearly highlighted the double standard that Red Shirt leaders had lamented all along. Reactionaries can shoot people in the streets, run police officers over with their trucks, riot in front of Parliament, trash Government House, and occupy the airports for a week with the impunity characteristically accorded in Thailand to the champions of the establishment. But if one stands against the aristocrats and the generals, shattering the glass doors of a five-star hotel is all it takes to be branded an enemy of the state.

The luck of the Red Shirts turned in a matter of hours, as the movement's leadership quickly lost control of the situation. Supporters scattered all over Bangkok resorted to desperate measures to halt the army's methodical advance. The height of irresponsibility was reached as Red Shirts commandeered LPG tankers and drove them into highly populated areas such as the Din Daeng triangle and Soi Rangnam, as if to threaten the annihilation of entire neighborhoods should the army dare to move in. To protect themselves, at least some of the Red Shirts had proven willing to endanger the lives of regular people — those whose interests and aspirations they ostensibly advance, those whose support is indispensable to the success of the movement. In the process, they squandered any good will the local population might have harbored towards them — reducing, for the time being, the prospects of a popular uprising to a mere pipe-dream.

There is little doubt, as the Red Shirt leaders alleged, that at least some of the disorder was instigated by *agents provocateurs* in an attempt to drive a wedge between the protesters and local residents. The tapes where Abhisit can be heard ordering unknown underlings to foment disorder were almost certainly doctored — the idea that Abhisit would *order* men with guns to do anything, in particular, seems ridiculous on its face. But it was hard to imagine those conversations did not take place, considering that the Thai government has routinely employed such strategies to great effect in the past. Anarchy, after all, is a dictator's best friend. Still, the Red Shirts took the bait.

As they increasingly lost control of their own people, the Red Shirts quickly succumbed to the media onslaught that accompanied the regime's crackdown. Given the Thai military's history of mass murder, it is difficult to fathom that anyone would believe a word that comes out of a general's mouth. But the government successfully disseminated its self-serving narrative nonetheless, portraying its actions as deliberate, orderly, and restrained in the face of an unwieldy, riotous mob. The servile local media eagerly obliged; the foreign press swallowed it whole. Of course, the official version of events was the usual pack of lies and half-truths. Photographs and video contradicted the preposterous notion that soldiers merely fired warning shots in the air, or that the weapons seen firing directly into the crowds had only been loaded with blank rounds. Certainly, the two bodies that surfaced, bound and mutilated, from the Chao Phraya River in the days following the disturbances appeared to suggest that there was more to the story than the authorities had conceded.[9]

By the afternoon of April 13, the Red Shirts had lost much of their support, their message, and their claim to "democratic" legitimacy. Their numbers vastly diminished, their

---

9. Piyaporn Wongruang and Aekarach Sattaburuth, "Questions Still Remain Over Bodies Found in Chao Phraya River," *Bangkok Post*, April 26, 2009.

resources depleted, their credibility in tatters, it would have been suicidal to lead the remaining protesters into a showdown with the army. And so, in the end, they just packed their bags and left. Clutching water bottles, walking slowly towards the buses aboard which they would begin the journey home, the Red Shirts streaming out of the encircled Government House looked more like a football team's vanquished supporters than revolutionaries forced to surrender by a violent government crackdown. Dejected and emotionally spent, to be sure, but still walking away from it with their lives, their limbs, and their freedom.

The failure of the Songkhran rebellion demonstrated that the Red Shirts could not yet count on the support of the key swing constituency — Bangkok's masses of ordinary people. Characteristically, it is Bangkok's millions-strong army of secretaries, clerks, accountants, shopkeepers, professionals, and students that will ultimately decide the fate of the old order. But the time had not yet come. For the most part, middle-income people in Bangkok remained on the fence, a posture reflecting the insecurity that has come to exemplify the petite bourgeoisie in times of uncertainty, conflict, and change. On the one hand, many middle-income Thais could easily identify with the Red Shirts' demands for democracy, equality under the law, and economic opportunity. On the other hand, not unlike their European counterparts during the interwar period, over the past several years urban middle class voters have repeatedly been warned that the masses' political inclusion will come largely at their expense.[10]

Thanks to its guns, its money, its magic, and its traditional stranglehold on the media, the old order lived on. The military, the palace, and the urban elites still had the population's apathy on their side — not to mention that the Thai people understandably had little taste for the kind of chaos the establishment had unleashed upon the country in the fall of 2008. What is more, Thaksin's coalition may now have been

---
10. For an illustration, see Pasuk and Baker, *Thaksin*, pp. 264-266.

irreparably fractured. But those who yearned for real democratic change — those whose ideals transcended the restoration of Thaksin to an office he occupied legitimately and abused shamefully — could take heart in the realization that the events leading up to the Songkhran rebellion had already undone decades of establishment propaganda. Old taboos had been shattered. Old myths had been demolished. And, at long last, the iniquity of old untouchables had increasingly been exposed to well-deserved public disgust.

The Red Shirts would be back soon enough. In the months that followed the April 2009 crackdown, the UDD went back to the hard work of recruiting followers, educating sympathizers, and building an organization in the provinces. In record time, these efforts catapulted the movement into one of the largest in the history of Thailand. And while the Red Shirts never quite got around to distancing themselves from Thaksin, their activities went a long way towards establishing a separate identity for the movement, decisively leading it out of the long shadow cast by the former Prime Minister. Less than a year after the failure of the Songkhran rebellion, the UDD announced it was launching its final battle against dictatorship, unveiling an ambitious plan to get a million people from all over the country to converge on Bangkok beginning on March 12, 2010.

In the face of the renewed groundswell of Red Shirt mobilization, the government almost instinctively exhumed some of the anti-communist rhetoric of the Cold War era. While some ridiculed the notion that a movement in part inspired and financed by a billionaire former Prime Minister could wage a "class war" on behalf of farmers and workers,[11] other government officials spoke openly of the "Maoist tactics"[12]

---

11. "Abhisit Questions Thaksin's Role as Leader of 'Class War'," *The Nation*, March 20, 2010.
12. See Pravit Rojanaphruk, "Reds Plan to Paralyze Bangkok, Topple Government: Sources," *The Nation*, March 9, 2010.

and "Marxist-Leninist ideology"[13] presumably inspiring the UDD.

These labels, of course, have been used many times before to brand movements for democracy as dangerous or un-Thai. But the Red Shirts, whatever one thinks of their motives, their leaders, or their grievances, have put forth demands that bear a much closer resemblance to a civil rights movement than to the vanguard of a "class struggle." More than it is about class, the Red Shirts movement is about identity — an identity defined on the basis of class as well as language, ethnicity, and regional origin, traits that variously combine to confer upon a sizable chunk of the population *de facto* second class citizenship status. More than economic redistribution, the Red Shirt movement is powered by demands for recognition and political inclusion — demands long frustrated by a privileged minority's insistence upon selecting the nation's leaders over the majority's wishes. More than poverty and economic hardship, what has made the Red Shirt movement possible was the new sense of empowerment acquired thanks to economic modernization — it was this new collective self-image as equal citizens that rendered the latest series of prevarications suffered at the hands of the palace, the military, and the urban elites no longer endurable. More than a unifying ideology founded upon economic equality, the Red Shirts share a simple vision of Thailand as a "normal" and possibly "democratic" country — one where elections have consequences and the law applies to everyone irrespective of wealth, status, or karmic stock.

The rediscovery of the word *phrai* as a label and an identifier, in this sense, not only clarified the nature of Red Shirts' struggle, but also brought into sharper focus just how radical a challenge — and how grave a threat — the Red Shirts had grown to present for Thailand's entrenched structure of power. Up until 1905, the word *phrai* referred to commoners at

---

13. See Shaun Tandon, "Thai Government Tells US It's in Charge," *Agence France-Presse*, June 11, 2010.

the lowest rung of Siamese social hierarchy (*sakdina*) — still free, but liable to *corvée* in the service of either the king, the army, or an individual landlord. The embracement of their identity as *phrai*, then, reflected not only the Red Shirts' newfound sense of pride in their status as commoners, but perhaps most ominously their rejection of an entire social order founded upon supposedly "natural" hierarchies of status and merit. Taking pride in low social status, in particular, highlighted the fact that many among them no longer accept the legitimacy of a social order founded on the myth that high status means "goodness" and "goodness" legitimizes privileged access to political power.

Whatever the government might say, this has never been a "class war." The fight is about restoring the palace to the ceremonial role it formally accepted, at the barrel of a gun, on June 24, 1932. Perhaps more importantly, the fight is about subjecting the *amarthaya* — the king's courtiers, mandarins, and praetorian guards, most themselves commoners by birth, who have long exploited the pretense of defending the monarchy to hoard power and riches for themselves — to the will of the people.

In the run-up to the demonstrations planned for March 2010, before a packed house at the Foreign Correspondents' Club of Thailand, acting government spokesman Panitan Wattanayagorn provided some unique insights into the anguish shared by much of Thailand's increasingly besieged political establishment in the face of this epochal challenge. After warning the Red Shirt representatives in attendance that, if pushed hard enough, the government would not hesitate to claim more expansive, "unaccountable" powers, Panitan allowed flashes of sincerity to percolate through an otherwise dissembling presentation on the country's ongoing political crisis. "What happened to us?" — he wondered aloud, an expression of disbelief on his face — "what happened to our patience, to our tolerance, to *mai pen rai*?"

Thailand's ruling class has never taken a *mai pen rai* approach to challenges to its authority. So it was hard to escape the conclusion that Panitan could not have been lamenting the change he had observed in the posture of generals, royals, privy councilors, politicians, and crony capitalists. His dismay could only have been directed at the vast majority of the Thai public, at those who have long been expected to turn the other cheek to violence, injustice, and exploitation. It is only their refusal to accept the latest usurpation of their power that could now lead the noted *sakdina* intellectual to profess his bewilderment.

Not five decades ago, political scientist David Wilson described Thai society in terms that offer a window into the source of Panitan's bemusement. Back then, Wilson observed "a clear distinction between those who are involved in politics and those who are not," adding that "the overwhelming majority of the adult population is not." He went on to say::

> The peasantry as the basic productive force constitutes more than eighty percent of the population and is the foundation of the social structure. But its inarticulate acquiescence to the central government and indifference to national politics are fundamental to the political system. A tolerable economic situation which provides a stable subsistence without encouraging any great hope for quick improvement is no doubt the background of this political inaction.[14]

Writing on the heels of Sarit's conservative revolution, Wilson was correct to identify in the "acquiescence" and "indifference" of the vast majority of the public the basis of "Thai-Style Democracy." Indeed, it was in the interest of building this system of government that Sarit had insisted that the provincial masses belonged in the fields. It was in the interest of preserving this system of government that His Majesty the King urged the Thai people to "walk backwards

---

16. David Wilson, *Politics in Thailand* (Ithaca: Cornell University Press, 1962).

into a *khlong*" and renounce progress in favor of a simple existence founded on economic sufficiency.[15] And it was in the interest of reiterating what this system of government once expected of them that Prime Minister Abhisit Vejjajiva most recently promised that everything would be fine, so long as the Thai people continued to "do their jobs lawfully.[16]" In a "Sufficiency Democracy," as Andrew Walker[17] calls it, a good citizen is not just satisfied with whatever life has given; just as important, a real Thai accepts to play a political role commensurate to his or her stock of accumulated merit — conveniently measured on the basis of one's *existing* wealth, social status, and political power.

"Thai-Style (Sufficiency) Democracy" was not destroyed in one day. Despite increasingly desperate pleas to be content with what they have, over time the people of Thailand have had enough of a "stable subsistence" and have flocked to Bangkok to fulfill dreams their leaders said they should not dare harbor. Economic growth and modernization did give rise to hopes that a "quick" and decisive "improvement" in their material condition would soon be within their grasp. Confronted with the refusal by the country's ruling class to grant them a fair share of the country's newfound prosperity — reliably built on the backs of the people — they shed their "indifference" and began to vote, *en masse*, for those who at least bothered to pay some lip service to their empowerment, who made them feel like they mattered. And when their will was overturned, not once but three times over the last four years, for many among them "acquiescence" was quite simply no longer an option. *Mai pen rai* has turned into *mai yom rap*.

For a variety of reasons — not the least of which is the

---

15. See Pasuk Phongpaichit, "Developing Social Alternatives: Walking Backwards into a *khlong*," in *Thailand Beyond the Crisis*, ed. Peter Warr (London: Routledge, 2005), p. 161.
16. Wassana Nanuam, "Abhisit Calls in Media to Slam Thaksin," *Bangkok Post*, March 20, 2010.
17. Andrew Walker, "Sufficiency Democracy," *New Mandala*, October 4, 2006.

arrogance of its guardians — "Thai-Style (Sufficiency) Democracy" has been in failing health for almost two decades. It finally died some time between March 12 and March 14, 2010, overpowered by the tens of thousands of people who marched on Bangkok to demand equality, justice, and "real" democracy. On March 20, its corpse was paraded through the city in a festive, fifty-kilometer-long procession attended by hundreds of thousands of people — what amounted to an unmistakably Thai rendition of a New Orleans jazz funeral.

In retrospect, the Red Shirts could never hope to bring a million people to Bangkok, given the monumental logistical challenges that would have presented under the best of circumstances. At the end of the day, their numbers were depressed further by the fact that these were not the best of circumstances. Thanks, in part, to the complicity of their own, most dimwitted leaders, in advance of their "final battle against dictatorship" the Red Shirts were successfully portrayed as barbarian, "rural hordes" — most of them paid, some of them brainwashed, many among them not really Thai — determined to lay waste to the capital city in a last-ditch effort to rescue the dwindling fortunes of one man. Just in case the widely anticipated prospects of violence and chaos (periodically revitalized by well-timed police raids and mysterious bomb attacks) had failed to scare enough people into staying home, hundreds of tripwires were laid down in the form of checkpoints extending deep into the Isan countryside. Then, just at the opportune time, the government pressed the panic button when it imposed the Internal Security Act and began speaking openly about the possibility of invoking the Emergency Decree — what would later amount, in practice, to an *autogolpe*.

And yet they came — not in large enough numbers to inaugurate a new system of government, to be sure, but in numbers certainly large enough to trample the old one to death. Some argued, with merit, that their motives remained diverse, their demands inarticulate, their strategy underdeveloped, and their leadership coarse, homophobic, and hopelessly divided against itself. Still, the death of the old system required no clear agenda, no unanimity of motive, no strategic acumen, and no enlightened leader; indeed, it did not even require the physical removal of Abhisit's puppet regime. What definitively snuffed the life out of "Thai-Style Democracy" is that its foundation of indifference and sheepish acquiescence had been thoroughly dismantled.

Assembled at two symbolically charged locations in downtown Bangkok — at Saphan Phan Fa and later at the Rajprasong intersection, surrounded by some of the world's most dazzling shopping malls — the Red Shirts spent weeks force-feeding the hapless Prime Minister repeated samplings of his own medicine. They defied the Internal Security Act as well as regulations issued pursuant to the Emergency Decree — invoked for no other reason than to allow Abhisit to continue his poor impersonation of a statesman, wholly dedicated to the rule of law, while simultaneously giving him the power to make up the law as he went along. They had performed transfixing Brahmanical cursing rituals, spilling human blood at the Prime Minister's residence, at the Government House, and at Democrat Party headquarters. Time and time again, they crossed every line in the sand that the government had drawn by declaring various locations in the city off-limits to their marches. They had entered the grounds of the National Assembly, forced their way into the building that houses the Election Commission, and stormed the Thaicom station in Patum Thani in an attempt to re-establish the People Channel's satellite signal. Perhaps most vexing of all, for a government that had spent weeks warning of grave security threats, the Red Shirts had been overwhelmingly peaceful, charming, and good humored. Security forces were frequently seen fraternizing with the demonstrators, whose forays around the city regularly attracted the sympathy of throngs of local residents.

By April 10, the government had seen quite enough. Having spent nearly a month hunkered down in his rathole at the Eleventh Regiment, protected by layers of razor wire and thousands of soldiers, Prime Minister Abhisit Vejjajiva had taken enough humiliation. The operations would be carried out by troops armed to the teeth, seemingly better equipped for a battle with an invading army than the dispersal of a crowd of mostly unarmed protesters. As the soldiers advanced towards the demonstration site at Saphan Phan Fa, on foot and in armored personnel vehicles, the government publicly boasted that "order" would be restored by nightfall.

But things would turn out differently this time. This time, the demonstrators — the vast majority armed with rocks, sticks, the occasional firebomb, and whatever they could find on the pavement that could be thrown at the security forces — refused to offer themselves as the inert victims of another state massacre. This time, the demonstrators fought back, with breathtaking courage, against the same kind of military regime that violently suppressed every democratic movement Thailand has ever known.

As the street battles unfolded, thousands of people continued to stream into the Red Shirt rallies, laying down their lives before the army's advance. Red Shirt leaders, whom the government had so often dismissed as charlatans and opportunists, did not shirk from their responsibility to lead the resistance against the violent crackdown. Whether they were motivated by old intramural grudges or active support of the Red Shirts, perhaps not more than a handful of men dressed in black — suspected to have been themselves military officers — assassinated the operation's commander, Col. Romklao Thuwatham, and some of his lieutenants before vanishing back into the shadows. Shockingly, it quickly became clear that butchering a couple dozen people would not be enough to silence the Red Shirts. This time, there would be no taking it lying down. Ceasefire.

The botched crackdown left twenty-six people dead — twenty-one protesters, four military officers, and a foreign journalist. A few days later, the Red Shirts abandoned their encampment at Saphan Phan Fa and concentrated their forces at Rajprasong. By retreating behind the barricades of a fortified compound in the heart of the city, the Red Shirts lost the mobility and adaptiveness that had enabled them to repeatedly embarrass the government over the previous weeks. But the move also placed the government in an impossible position. On the one hand, the occupation of an area of far greater commercial significance than Rachadamnoen Avenue put Abhisit's government under increased pressure from its own supporters to bring the demonstrations to a close. As the government wavered, coalition politicians grumbled, while the increasingly hysterical People's Alliance for Democracy slammed the failure to put down the Red Shirts whatever the cost. On the other hand, it would have been obvious to anyone who had ever taken a stroll across Red Shirt City at Rajprasong that their dispersal may not only have required a bloodbath evocative of the Paris Commune, but perhaps more importantly to lay waste to some of Bangkok's most iconic developments. And the Red Shirts understood that, in this day and age, Louis Vuitton bags and Hermès foulards make for better shields than human shields.

Whether by choice or compelled by the military's refusal to carry out his orders, Abhisit offered to dissolve the House within four months, a decision that would presumably have paved the way for an election in November 2010. It might be worth asking how significant an accomplishment a November election might have been for the Red Shirts. Earlier, in late March, Abhisit himself had publicly stated his readiness to dissolve the House in nine months. Had it been worth holding out, at the cost of thirty additional lives, for a three-to-six-month discount on the proposed election timeline? Or were the Red Shirts now compelled to press ahead, if they were to honor the memory of their dead? These questions were animatedly debated in the Red Shirt camp, as their leaders pondered a response.

Those arguing in favor of accepting the offer could point out that the Red Shirts had accomplished a great deal since the breakdown of the televised "negotiations" with the Prime Minister held in late March. The myriad provocations that the Red Shirts successfully carried out had not only exposed the dreadful incompetence of the country's security forces, but also brought to the surface some troubling rifts within the military itself. Perhaps most importantly, by then the Red Shirts had all but defaced the most handsome, mild-mannered, soft-spoken, and fiercely amoral facade available to the country's royalist establishment. To many among those who did not like him to begin with, Abhisit was now a murderer whose hands were covered in the people's blood. To many among those who had no firm opinion, Abhisit was just the last in a long series of weak Prime Ministers at the mercy of people and institutions he could never really hope to control. And, to many among those who enthusiastically supported his rise to power, Abhisit was a coward whose failure to take decisive action bordered on treason.

Under siege and seemingly in the throes of unharnessed desperation, the Prime Minister had played the "protect the monarchy" card from the bottom of the deck — alleging a fanciful conspiracy illustrated by the now infamous diagram that Colonel Sansern Kaewkamnerd handed out to reporters. This could have been a blunder of potentially career-ending proportions. Manufacturing an existential threat to the nation might have served as a convenient excuse for mass murder. But if one is unable or unwilling to massacre hundreds of people, it is inevitable that those who believed the charges, or in any event found it convenient to hype the allegations, will judge the refusal to confront an existential threat head on as tantamount to dereliction of duty, if not out-and-out complicity.

Still, the offer placed the Red Shirts before a difficult dilemma. On the one hand, rejecting the deal was sure to make them appear unreasonable to many among those who had remained "neutral" throughout this fight — perhaps especially, those urban middle class voters the UDD had worked so hard to court ever since it set up camp on the streets of Bangkok. On the other hand, Abhisit's offer came with no guarantees. To accept it without conditions would have meant for the Red Shirts to suspend their rally in exchange for promises many suspected to be empty.

For one thing, questions remained over whether Abhisit could credibly commit to keep up his own end of the bargain. Considerable uncertainty, in particular, surrounded the outcome of two Constitutional Court rulings on the possible dissolution of the Democrat Party. It was unclear at the time whether the timing of the Election Commission's decision to refer the long-delayed cases to the Constitutional Court was mere coincidence, whether it was designed to induce the Prime Minister to leave or remind him he answered to higher powers, or whether it was merely a cheap trick to deflate the Red Shirts' outrage against perceived "double standards." It was only much later, in December 2010, that the Constitutional Court finally dismissed the charges on a technicality. Considering, moreover, that Thailand was now under the worst censorship regime since the days that followed the 1976 massacre, there would not be anything like a "free and fair election" so long as this kind of government stayed in office — it mattered little who served as the executive's titular head. And despite the lip service paid by the Prime Minister to the need to investigate the deaths on April 10, everyone knows that human rights abuses on this scale have never received any proper investigation in Thailand, much less any real justice.

The UDD leadership sought to thread the needle by outwardly embracing Abhisit's so-called "roadmap for reconciliation" conditional upon two guarantees one would be hard-pressed to describe as unreasonable — the relaxation of censorship and the launch of an independent investigation into the April 10 incidents. The third condition — that

Deputy Prime Minister Suthep Thaugsuban turn himself him to acknowledge criminal charges the police had not yet filed — seemed more specifically designed to derail the entire process. The Red Shirts effectively threw the ball back into Abhisit's court. The Prime Minister, his escape routes now blocked, would now have to pick his poison. His options were limited to dissolving the House, and hence commit political suicide, or crack down so ruthlessly as to not only self-destruct, but possibly bring the entire regime he represented down with him.

A few days passed, more deadlines to comply with the government's long series of ultimatums came and went, but in the end the operation was a go. Abhisit took his offer of an early election off the table as troops and armored personnel carriers gradually encircled Rajprasong. The first shot, fired by a sniper, rang out on May 13, assassinating the rogue Major-General Khattiya Sawasdipol. In the following days, the carnage unfolded as battles raged at Din Daeng and along on the southern edge of Lumphini Park. Ever obsessed with the appearance of urbanity, the government placed signs designating "Live Fire Zones" — more accurately, "free fire zones" where the military had essentially been given carte blanche to shoot civilians, journalists, and emergency medical personnel. After days of fighting, the siege successfully softened the UDD's resistance, while the savagery exhibited by the government against its own citizens depressed the number of protesters left at Rajprasong.

On the morning of May 19, the army easily overrode the Red Shirt barricades and penetrated their encampment. Faced with the certainty of defeat, the movement's leaders saved their own lives and those of perhaps dozens of their followers, many apparently determined to fight to the death, by waving the white flag. The surrender had to be announced in haste. Before they could persuade the weeping, jeering crowds of the wisdom of retreating, shots rang out and the Red Shirt leaders ducked for cover, scrambling to leave the stage and reach the safety of the nearby police station. Now leaderless, some of those left in the streets took out their anger and disappointment on some targets of opportunity and a few others of symbolic significance, setting a number of buildings ablaze as they scattered throughout the city.

In a strictly tactical sense, the operation proved to be a success. Though it was never in doubt that a modern army, even one as incompetent, would eventually defeat a few thousand protesters protected by several dozen lightly armed men, the final push produced far fewer casualties than many had feared — less than sixty people are officially said to have died in the days since Seh Daeng's assassination. But even the government could not bring itself to describe the operation's success as a victory. No government has ever drawn much in the way of a long-term benefit from a carnage of this magnitude. Besides reclaiming two or three square kilometers of prime real estate, at the total cost of ninety-one lives, the operation solved none of the current regime's fatal structural flaws. And the extreme measures that the government was forced to take by the Red Shirts — the Emergency Decree, the suspension of civil and political rights, the suppression of most alternative sources of information, and the establishment of a new organ, the Center for the Resolution of the Emergency Situation (CRES), bearing an uncanny resemblance to a hurriedly cobbled-up junta in the mold of Burma's SLORC — wrecked the democratic appearances Abhisit had once taken great care to keep up. To defeat a movement that objected to its illegitimacy and authoritarianism, the government had to fully reveal itself as such.

Certainly, the Red Shirts did not emerge from Rajprasong looking especially good either. Thanks to their leaders' decision to surrender, their last stand did not turn out like the Paris Commune. Still, they lost more than fifty additional people. Their support among middle class voters in Bangkok and some of the surrounding provinces was be compromised by their intransigence as well as the property damage inflicted in the wake of their surrender. Their leaders were arrested and faced far more serious charges as a result of having forced Abhisit to murder more of their people. In addition, the arson attacks committed by some of their followers provided the government — and Thailand's eagerly compliant media — with just the sort of apocalyptic images it needed to further dehumanize the Red Shirts, ignore the pile of corpses sacrificed on the altar of smoother traffic and a more satisfying shopping experience, and at least in the short run provide retroactive justification for the killings.

Then again, nothing was lost — only the latest victims of state violence and civilian complacency would never come back. The movement's support remained strong. In the North and the Northeast as among the urban underclasses, supporters were not likely to shed any tears over the fact that some rich punk in Bangkok could no longer shop at Central World, when dozens of people like them lay dead at the hands of the government. If anything, those who already sympathized with the Red Shirts reacted with justifiable disgust at the sight of upper- and upper-middle-class citizens in Bangkok making such a scene out of mourning the loss of a shopping mall — whose burning was compared, laughably, to September 11, 2001 — while they continued to shrug off (and, in many cases, celebrate) the murder of so many people.

Earlier promises to the contrary notwithstanding, this was nothing close to a "final battle." Indeed, given that the million-strong crowds never materialized, this was a battle that would certainly not have been final even if the Red Shirts had ultimately won it. To borrow imagery from Nattawut Saikua's stirring speech, however, the sky is closer today than it has ever been. The old order is dead. Those who would seek to restore it are badly wounded. And while the star of its big-time players is fading fast, the establishment's bench is not deep on charisma, competence, and legitimacy. Most important of all, the Red Shirts have already conquered that once-elusive "rightful place" where they can firmly "plant their feet," having busted down the gates of a political system from which ordinary people have long been excluded. The Red Shirts have already seized for themselves the right to be "Thai" by colorfully rejecting their old status as second-class citizens. To those inhabiting both the earth and the sky, who so often described them as corruptible and unprincipled, they have already shown the strength of their hearts and the fortitude of their souls. Having shattered a once impenetrable noise barrier of censorship and indifference, their deafening cries swamp the high heavens.

> If one is to rule, and to continue ruling, one must be able to dislocate the sense of reality. For the secret of rulership is to combine a belief in one's own infallibility with the power to learn from past mistakes.
>
> —GEORGE ORWELL
> *Nineteen Eighty-Four*

SEVEN

TWILIGHT OF THE IDOLS

> The other old man laughed softly. 'The flowers of democracy blossom and fade, but new blooms will always replace the old. What else can you expect from this good old world of ours, except the one truth, that nothing is forever.'
>
> —WIN LYOVARIN[1]

The streets of Bangkok have long served as the theater where the Thai people's struggle for democracy turns into real-life tragedy. At varying intervals since the early 1970s, tens of thousands of demonstrators have taken to the streets of Bangkok to demand that the country's government finally live up to its official, "democratic" billing. Whenever perceived as a real threat to the survival of a less than democratic regime, the demonstrators have been met with the full brunt of military force, which tends to be especially fierce when the power and perquisites of army's chieftains hang in the balance.

The state massacres that have taken hundreds of innocent lives in 1973, 1976, 1992, and 2010 are variations on the same theme. Demonstrations menacing enough to elicit a brutal crackdown were invariably sparked off by events that

---

1. Win Lyovarin, *Democracy, Shaken and Stirred* (Bangkok: 113 Company Ltd., 2003), p. 9.

stripped bare the country's fraudulent pretense of "democracy." In response, the government laid the groundwork for a violent response by portraying the demonstrators as traitors and radicals, whose cries for freedom masked more sinister designs to destroy the monarchy.

Whether or not the state's propaganda machine succeeded in turning the demonstrators into a threat to everything Thailand holds dear, the blood still flowed all the same. The public's reaction to the carnage, however, would come to define the manner in which the establishment cleaned up its own mess. Whenever the massacre was met with horror in Bangkok, as it was in 1973 and in 1992, King Bhumibol stepped in to prevent any lasting damage to the image of the palace and preserve the integrity of the system. In both instances, the officials most tainted by the violence symbolically took the fall, but were ushered out of office gently under guarantees of impunity, promises of royally-sponsored funerals honoring their services to a higher cause, and/or lucrative careers in the private sector. When the public in the capital largely shrugged off the killings, as it did in 1976 and 2010, Ramkhamhaeng's bell conveniently fell silent. In both of these instances, King Bhumibol would have nothing to say about the atrocities carried out in his name.

The massacres that repeatedly soaked the city of Bangkok in the blood of Thai citizens from all walks of life may share a similar plot, but not the same historical import. Activist Sombat Boonngamanong puts it rather succinctly:

> I believe this will be the last fight. All the revolutions in Thailand are about sharing the power and status. The 1932 revolution was for the military, 1973 and 1976 were for intellectuals, 1992 was for the middle class. This time, it will be for ordinary people.[2]

While the "last fight" Sombat refers to has in all likelihood

---

2. Monruedee Jansuttipan, "How Red Shirt Activist Sees a Revolution to End All Revolutions," *BK*, December 16, 2010.

only just begun, the demonstrations staged by Red Shirt protesters between March and May 2010 have marked the end of an era for Thailand — the end of "Thai-Style Democracy," a five-decades-old system of government that, notwithstanding the appropriation of some of the trappings of democracy, has largely preserved the right of "good" men of high birth, status, and wealth to run the country. Whereas the prolonged rallies notably failed to achieve their immediate objective — to bring down the government of Prime Minister Abhisit Vejjajiva — the hundreds of thousands of people who marched on Bangkok, many belonging to constituencies whose right to participate in the country's government has never before been acknowledged, thoroughly dismantled the foundations of a system of government built on the acquiescence and indifference of the vast majority of the Thai public.

In the wake of what was, at least by the official estimates, the deadliest episode of repression of pro-democracy demonstrators in the history of Thailand, Abhisit promised "reconciliation." Just in case the details of the Prime Minister's "roadmap" had not made this perfectly clear, the actions that his government took since the dispersal of the Red Shirt rallies on May 19 erased any doubts that what Abhisit meant by "reconciliation" is neither accountability nor the resolution of substantive differences by way of compromise. In the government's usage, "reconciliation" meant "restoration" — the restoration of the Thai people's lost acquiescence, the restoration of their innocence from the taint of foreign ideas like "democracy," "equality," and "progress."

The call to "protect the monarchy," in particular, is in keeping with the old Saritian tradition of borrowing the government's legitimacy from the throne, while the witch-hunt in progress to root out a phantom conspiracy to overthrow the King underscores its determination to perpetuate the five-decades-old habit of branding the government's enemies as closet republicans. The promise to address some of the economic grievances of the Red Shirts, while ignoring their demands for political inclusion, reflects the establishment's conviction that a few handouts might just be enough to bribe their sympathizers into abandoning the fight for their civil and political rights. The commitment to making the media into a "constructive tool" — by censoring news outlets reporting less "constructive" facts as well as by educating the public to make "correct use" of new media — exemplifies the same paternalistic arrogance exhibited by each of Thailand's past military regimes. Finally, if Abhisit's attempt to whitewash the latest episode of state violence aimed to extend to himself and his colleagues the cover of impunity enjoyed by those who carried out similar massacres in 1973, 1976, and 1992, his campaign to disguise the cover-up as an "independent investigation" exposed his government's unfailing contempt for the intelligence of its citizens.

Perhaps the best evidence of the government's reactionary designs, nonetheless, is offered by the extreme repression with which it has felt necessary to complement its "roadmap" for reconciliation. On the strength of its sweeping new powers, Abhisit's administration went on to oversee the most heavy-handed attempt to silence voices of dissent in a generation; those media outlets not censored were enlisted in a massive propaganda campaign to prop up the government and destroy the opposition. After presiding over the killing of ninety-one people, just to recapture a few square kilometers of prime real estate in central Bangkok from largely unarmed protesters, Abhisit pursued the Red Shirts relentlessly. Over four hundred were arrested — some held without charge, others tried and convicted at lightning speed, still others put on trial on terrorism charges leading to possible death sentences. Meanwhile, seemingly every week, citizens are arrested on suspicion of lèse majesté and "computer crimes," accusations that have fast become the regime's weapon of choice to censor, punish, and deter opposition to its rule.

These measures suggest that Abhisit's government never had the ambition to bring about meaningful "reconciliation."

But if the idea that reconciliation will be achieved on a foundation of repression and impunity is nonsensical enough, the government's "roadmap for restoration" — to re-educate the skeptical, terrorize the reticent, and crush the undaunted — may turn out to be no less fanciful.

Over the course of its half-century life span, "Thai-Style Democracy" successfully adapted in response to at least two major disruptions comparable to the one constituted by the assertion of Thai Rak Thai's electoral dominance. In both prior instances, successful adaptation was preceded by attempts at restoration — attempts whose failure offers valuable clues about the prospects faced by the effort that is currently underway.

The 1976 coup that installed Tanin Kraivichien's despotic regime in the immediate wake of the gruesome massacre of dozens of Thammasat University students marked an attempt to restore Thailand to the days of Thanom and Prapat, if not Sarit, after the chaotic period of "real" democracy ushered in by the 1973 protests. Even the extreme repression unleashed by Tanin, however, could not bring back "Thai-Style Democracy" in its original, Saritian form — a form devoid of meaningful political rights and representative institutions. Failed restoration gave way to adaptation. The solution was "Premocracy," a hybridized form of government that combined elements of democracy with features of the old system. On the one hand, the palace conserved its dominance over Thailand's political system, which had been achieved over the course of the 1970s — for eight years, the King ruled by proxy through an unelected Prime Minister, the trusted General Prem Tinsulanonda. On the other hand, the failure of the virtual "theocracy" inaugurated after the 1976 massacre inspired an ideological shift that sought to boost the stability of the system by emphasizing the unity of the King and the peasantry.[3] It is on this basis that the His Majesty's avowedly retrograde ideas of "sufficiency" would later be founded.

---

3. See Streckfuss, *The Truth on Trial in Thailand*, pp. 213-215.

Similarly, Suchinda's 1991 coup marked an attempt to restore Thailand to the days of "Premocracy" after Chatichai Choonhavan's two-and-a-half-year tenure as Prime Minister — an attempt to turn back the clock to a time when an unelected military man could govern Thailand, legitimized by the existence of a functioning parliament but not meaningfully encumbered by any changes elections might bring to its composition. That restoration failed, too, when tens of thousands of people rose up against Suchinda in May 1992. Once again, Suchinda's brutality could bring back that which had been already consigned to the history books. The solution was a new adaptation that satisfied the Thai people's wish to elect their own Prime Minister, but preserved the authority of unelected institutions to impose national policy through the manipulation of elected governments notorious for their weakness, fragmentation, and corruption.[4]

The failure of these prior instances of restoration does not bode well for Abhisit and his patrons. The lesson is that no amount of repression in the short term can restore the long-term stability of a social contract whose enforcement has outlasted the people's availability to honor it. The solution is either adaptation or more repression. The former, however, is complicated by the fact that "Thai-Style Democracy" has arguably run out of room to adapt. If, in particular, what prevented the 1992 protests from ushering in more sweeping political change was the indifference with which the demonstrations were received in rural Thailand, the political awakening of the rural population accomplished during Thaksin's tenure as Prime Minister has turned workers, farmers, and ordinary people in the provinces into the main threats to the establishment's power.

At the same time, further repression is rendered unthinkable as a long-term solution by the fact that what little popular legitimacy the government's authoritarian measures were

---

4. See Duncan McCargo, "Network Monarchy and Legitimacy Crises in Thailand," *Pacific Review* 18(2005): 499-519, pp. 507-515.

provisionally accorded in the wake of the crackdown is just one, increasingly faint, eighty-three-year-old heartbeat away from vanishing entirely. After the passing of King Bhumibol — the only member of the royal family who still commands some residual support, respect, and fear — it is difficult to imagine that large enough segments of the Thai public will accept the notion that the need to protect the monarchy justifies the continuing denial of majority rule and the periodic, arbitrary suspension of their civil and political rights.

While nobody quite knows what arrangement will take shape in the years to come, it is probably safe to say that the only chance of stability is offered by one that recognizes the people's right to govern their own country — something the citizens of Thailand, whether or not they sympathize with the Red Shirts, have repeatedly affirmed the eagerness and readiness to do. With or without the stewardship of the current set of officeholders, Thailand will eventually find real reconciliation in real democracy. It remains to be seen when, how, and at the expense of how many more lives.

At this point, the question is whether the Thai establishment is prepared to fight to the death, or whether it is open to eventually cutting a deal. Beyond the benefits that achieving a measure of "real" reconciliation sooner rather than later might have for the country as a whole, there are good reasons why Thailand's ruling class may want to cut a deal now. Perhaps most importantly, while Thailand may already have reached a point of no return, Thailand's monarchy — the keystone of the establishment — seems to be dangerously approaching its own. The 2006 coup may well have pushed Thaksin Shinawatra out of the way in time to prevent him from taking advantage of the King's death to dismantle the network of power His Majesty personifies, but only at the cost of putting the dynasty's entire future on the line.

The actions necessary to the removal of Thaksin and his proxies have given rise to a hitherto unseen measure of disgust for the royal family. Having made so little effort to conceal their support for the actions of the military, the judiciary, and the PAD against governments elected by the people, King Bhumibol and Queen Sirikit not only showed, yet again, their characteristic disdain for the democratic process, but perhaps most damagingly their contempt for the choices made by their own subjects. In the past, their contrived pretense of benign paternalism was enough to mask, offset, or rationalize their illiberal, anti-democratic views. But the elaborate pantomime, however well-funded, no longer works now that the people no longer accept to be treated as special needs children, and that the flow of information cannot be so easily controlled.

Indeed, while many in Thailand and in the foreign press have long been sold on the facile notion that the palace's stabilizing role has prevented the country from degenerating into even greater chaos and violence, it is becoming increasingly obvious that the monarchy is the main obstacle preventing Thailand from developing into normal, democratic country — something that many other former military dictatorship in Asia, Europe, and Latin America have managed to accomplish long ago. This, incidentally, is not exclusively attributable to the King's own actions — now frail and seemingly not in full control of either his movements or mental faculties, His Majesty himself is becoming irrelevant as an actual decision-maker. The reason is rather that the King's stultifying cult of personality continues to justify any abuse, any restriction, any prevarication, and any injustice inflicted in the supposed interest of protecting "the institution." Unless the monarchy finally modernizes, and reconciles itself to playing a purely ceremonial, constitutional role, Thailand's future as a normal, democratic country is unimaginable but for as a republic. Worse yet, as more and more people at home and abroad awaken to the reality that the monarchy *is* the problem, the window of opportunity available to the palace to pursue these reforms willingly is becoming smaller by the day.

It is difficult to tell, as Thitinan Pongsudhirak argued months ago, whether Abhisit ever really considered himself the "savior of the throne." Certainly, some skepticism is warranted in light of the fact that Abhisit is smart enough to know that the most dangerous threat to the monarchy is not posed by any tenebrous conspiracy, but rather by the continued misuse of the imperative to defend it as the excuse for extra-judicial executions, illegal detentions, political persecution, and military dictatorship. Indeed, the decision of its supposed defenders to double down on fanaticism, hatred, censorship, and repression is only turning the monarchy's preservation into an anachronism. Unlike their Prime Minister, for the most part the people of Thailand are no longer willing to prostrate themselves to the level of dogs. And so, in the not so distant future, the recent Red Shirt demonstrations could be remembered as merely the first ripple in what is a possible tsunami headed in the direction of Thailand's establishment — the kind of giant wave that wipes the House of Chakri off the face of the earth together with its loyal retinue of bitter-enders and *amarthaya*.

For the people of Thailand, the death of the old order, and the biological certainty that those who built it will not be far behind, offers a historic chance. A chance to take out the trash and slaughter the sacred cows. A chance to honor the distinctive traditions that make Thailand a unique, special place without subjecting dissenting views to censorship, legal harassment, or violence. A chance to reject the simplistic, vulgar reduction of Thai culture to the mere requirement that the most wretched always grovel before the most fortunate. A chance to recognize that tolerance, freedom, and non-violence are as integral a part of Thai culture as *sakdina*-based social hierarchy. A chance to restore Buddhism to more than just a convenient excuse for inequalities in power and wealth. A chance to bring the military under civilian control. A chance to come clean about the country's recent history. A chance to write a constitution that begins with an ideal in the stead of a lie. A chance to acknowledge that the story of the last seventy-five years is not the "development" of democratic institutions, but rather the establishment's increasingly desperate attempt to deny the people real democracy. A chance to pay homage to the sacrifice of those who died for democracy by telling the truth about their executioners. A chance to empower the people through equitable development, education, rights, and participation. A chance to lead Thailand into the developed world not through the back door of repression and exploitation, but as the nation of laws, freedom, justice, and opportunity it has always aspired to be.

Printed by BoD™ in Norderstedt, Germany